THE SELECTED POEMS OF FRANK O'HARA

THE SELECTED POEMS OF
FRANK O'HARA

EDITED BY DONALD ALLEN

VINTAGE BOOKS

A DIVISION OF RANDOM HOUSE   NEW YORK

First Vintage Books Edition January 1974

Copyright 1950, 1951, 1952, 1953, 1954, © 1955, 1956, 1957, 1958, 1959, 1960, 1961, 1962, 1964, 1965, 1966,
1967, 1968, 1969, 1970, 1971, 1973 by Maureen Granville-Smith, Administratrix of the Estate of Frank O'Hara.
All rights reserved under International and Pan-American Copyright Conventions.

Published in the United States by Random House, Inc., New York.

Distributed in Canada by Random House of Canada Limited, Toronto.

Originally published by Alfred A. Knopf, Inc., in January 1974.

Some of these poems first appeared in Angel Hair, Audit, "C," Ephemeris II, Evergreen Review,
Harper's Bazaar, The Harvard Advocate, The New American Poetry, The New Republic, The Paris Review,
Partisan Review, Poetry, San Francisco Earthquake, Texas Quarterly, Yūgen,
Locus Solus, Sum, Fathar, Adventures in Poetry, Folder, Accent, The Bonacker: A Collection of
Eastern Long Island Writing, Floating Bear, Generation, Hasty Papers, Second Coming, Swank.

Library of Congress Cataloging in Publication Data

O'Hara, Frank.   The selected poems of Frank O'Hara.

I. Allen, Donald Merriam, (date)   ed II. Title.

[PS3529.H28A6 1974b]   811'.5'4   73-7903

ISBN 0-394-71973-5

Manufactured in the United States of America

After devoting the better part of three years (five would have been even better) to the erection of the splendid palace known as *The Collected Poems of Frank O'Hara,* it at first seemed almost impossible to dismantle and reconstruct a selection. Fortunately my neighbor Bill Berkson came to the rescue; between us we managed to saw and hammer a possible structure. That was more than a year ago. Meanwhile, Kenneth Koch generously took a long look at our choices and gave us his certainties, doubts, and hesitations. Then Jimmy Schuyler added his suggestions, and our admirable editor Judith Jones added hers. Thus have we all together at last constructed *The Selected Poems.* Our grateful thanks to each and every one.

The overall arrangement of the poems remains chronological. We've added a brief chronology of Frank O'Hara's short life and an index of titles and first lines as aids to the reader.

D . A .

CONTENTS

PERSONISM: A MANIFESTO

Everything is in the poems, but at the risk of sounding like the poor wealthy man's Allen Ginsberg I will write to you because I just heard that one of my fellow poets thinks that a poem of mine that can't be got at one reading is because I was confused too. Now, come on. I don't believe in god, so I don't have to make elaborately sounded structures. I hate Vachel Lindsay, always have; I don't even like rhythm, assonance, all that stuff. You just go on your nerve. If someone's chasing you down the street with a knife you just run, you don't turn around and shout, "Give it up! I was a track star for Mineola Prep."

That's for the writing poems part. As for their reception, suppose you're in love and someone's mistreating (*mal aimé*) you, you don't say, "Hey, you can't hurt me this way, I care!" you just let all the different bodies fall where they may, and they always do may after a few months. But that's not why you fell in love in the first place, just to hang onto life, so you have to take your chances and try to avoid being logical. Pain always produces logic, which is very bad for you.

I'm not saying that I don't have practically the most lofty ideas of anyone writing today, but what difference does that make? They're just ideas. The only good thing about it is that when I get lofty enough I've stopped thinking and that's when refreshment arrives.

But how can you really care if anybody gets it, or gets what it means, or if it improves them. Improves them for what? For death? Why hurry them along? Too many poets act like a middle-aged mother trying to get her kids to eat too much cooked meat, and potatoes with drippings (tears). I don't give a damn whether they eat or not. Forced feeding leads to excessive thinness (effete). Nobody should experience anything they don't need to, if they don't need poetry bully for them. I like the movies too. And after all, only Whitman and Crane and Williams, of the American poets, are better than the movies. As for measure and other technical apparatus, that's just common sense: if you're going to buy a pair of pants you want them to be tight enough so everyone will want to go to bed with you. There's nothing metaphysical about it. Unless, of course, you flatter yourself into thinking that what you're experiencing is "yearning."

Abstraction in poetry, which Allen [Ginsberg] recently commented on in *It Is,* is intriguing. I think it appears mostly in the minute particulars where decision is necessary. Abstraction (in poetry, not in painting) involves personal removal by the poet. For instance, the decision involved in the choice between "the nostalgia *of* the infinite" and "the nostalgia *for* the infinite" defines an attitude towards degree of abstraction. The nostalgia *of* the infinite representing the greater degree of abstraction, removal, and negative capability (as in Keats and Mallarmé). Personism, a movement which I recently founded and which nobody knows about, interests me a great deal, being so totally opposed to this kind of abstract removal that it is verging on a true abstraction for the first time, really, in the history of poetry. Personism is to Wallace Stevens what *la poésie pure* was to Béranger. Personism has nothing to do with philosophy, it's all art. It does not have to do with personality or intimacy, far from it! But to give you a vague idea, one of its minimal aspects is to address itself to one person (other than the poet himself), thus evoking overtones of love without destroying love's life-giving vulgarity, and sustaining the poet's feelings towards the poem while preventing love from distracting him into feeling about the person. That's part of Personism. It was founded by me after lunch with LeRoi Jones on August 27, 1959, a day in which I was in love with someone (not Roi, by the way, a blond). I went back to work and wrote a poem for this person. While I was writing it I was realizing that if I wanted to I could use the telephone instead of writing the poem, and so Personism was born. It's a very exciting movement which will undoubtedly have lots of adherents. It puts the poem squarely between the poet and the person, Lucky Pierre style, and the poem is correspondingly gratified. The poem is at last between two persons instead of two pages. In all modesty, I confess that it may be the death of literature as we know it. While I have certain regrets, I am still glad I got there before Alain Robbe-Grillet did. Poetry being quicker and surer than prose, it is only just that poetry finish literature off. For a time people thought that Artaud was going to accomplish this, but actually, for all their magnificence, his polemical writings are not more outside literature than Bear Mountain is outside New York State. His relation is no more astounding than Debuffet's to painting.

What can we expect of Personism? (This is getting good, isn't it?) Everything, but we won't get it. It is too new, too vital a movement to promise anything. But it, like Africa, is on the way. The recent propagandists for technique on the one hand, and for content on the other, had better watch out.

September 3, 1959

Personism: A Manifesto

THE SELECTED POEMS OF FRANK O'HARA

AUTOBIOGRAPHIA LITERARIA

When I was a child
I played by myself in a
corner of the schoolyard
all alone.

I hated dolls and I
hated games, animals were
not friendly and birds
flew away.

If anyone was looking
for me I hid behind a
tree and cried out "I am
an orphan."

And here I am, the
center of all beauty!
writing these poems!
Imagine!

THE MUSE CONSIDERED AS A DEMON LOVER

Once at midnight in the fall
I woke with a shout at a light!

it burned all over the sheets, the
walls were panting with excitement!

a picture fell down! and a collage
peeled into a forest floor! It was

an angel! was I invited to a butterfly
ball? did it want to be in my movie?

It winked and took me by the hand:
"Max Ernst waits for us." "Petulant!"

it cried. It shrugged and listlessly
sat on my typewriter. The light went

out. "Que manges-tu, belle sphinx?"
came roaring through the dark; beau!

I muttered and hid my head, but a
wrenching kiss woke me again with a

"Suis-je belle, ô nausée?" We danced
in the light, that angel and I, sang

"Towards you all anguine conebos seem
to scoot"; oh I'd never let that angel

go! But seriously it said to me "I've
got to get a bun." My feet went blind.

The angel's voice called gaily: "There
are faith, hope, and charity, and

the greatest of these is homily. I
am an angel. Trouvez Hortense!"

POEM

At night Chinamen jump
on Asia with a thump

while in our willful way
we, in secret, play

affectionate games and bruise
our knees like China's shoes.

The birds push apples through
grass the moon turns blue,

these apples roll beneath
our buttocks like a heath

full of Chinese thrushes
flushed from China's bushes.

As we love at night
birds sing out of sight,

Chinese rhythms beat
through us in our heat,

the apples and the birds
move us like soft words,

we couple in the grace
of that mysterious race.

POEM

The eager note on my door said "Call me,
call when you get in!" so I quickly threw
a few tangerines into my overnight bag,
straightened my eyelids and shoulders, and

headed straight for the door. It was autumn
by the time I got around the corner, oh all
unwilling to be either pertinent or bemused, but
the leaves were brighter than grass on the sidewalk!

Funny, I thought, that the lights are on this late
and the hall door open; still up at this hour, a
champion jai-alai player like himself? Oh fie!
for shame! What a host, so zealous! And he was

there in the hall, flat on a sheet of blood that
ran down the stairs. I did appreciate it. There are few
hosts who so thoroughly prepare to greet a guest
only casually invited, and that several months ago.

TODAY

Oh! kangaroos, sequins, chocolate sodas!
You really are beautiful! Pearls,
harmonicas, jujubes, aspirins! all
the stuff they've always talked about

still makes a poem a surprise!
These things are with us every day
even on beachheads and biers. They
do have meaning. They're strong as rocks.

MEMORIAL DAY 1950

Picasso made me tough and quick, and the world;
just as in a minute plane trees are knocked down
outside my window by a crew of creators.
Once he got his axe going everyone was upset
enough to fight for the last ditch and heap
of rubbish.
                    Through all that surgery I thought
I had a lot to say, and named several last things
Gertrude Stein hadn't had time for; but then
the war was over, those things had survived
and even when you're scared art is no dictionary.
Max Ernst told us that.
                              How many trees and frying pans
I loved and lost! Guernica hollered look out!
but we were all busy hoping our eyes were talking
to Paul Klee. My mother and father asked me and
I told them from my tight blue pants we should
love only the stones, the sea, and heroic figures.
Wasted child! I'll club you on the shins! I
wasn't surprised when the older people entered
my cheap hotel room and broke my guitar and my can
of blue paint.
                    At that time all of us began to think
with our bare hands and even with blood all over

them, we knew vertical from horizontal, we never
smeared anything except to find out how it lived.
Fathers of Dada! You carried shining erector sets
in your rough bony pockets, you were generous
and they were lovely as chewing gum or flowers!
Thank you!

       And those of us who thought poetry
was crap were throttled by Auden or Rimbaud
when, sent by some compulsive Juno, we tried
to play with collages or sprechstimme in their bed.
Poetry didn't tell me not to play with toys
but alone I could never have figured out that dolls
meant death.

       Our responsibilities did not begin
in dreams, though they began in bed. Love is first of all
a lesson in utility. I hear the sewage singing
underneath my bright white toilet seat and know
that somewhere sometime it will reach the sea:
gulls and swordfishes will find it richer than a river.
And airplanes are perfect mobiles, independent
of the breeze; crashing in flames they show us how
to be prodigal. O Boris Pasternak, it may be silly
to call to you, so tall in the Urals, but your voice
cleans our world, clearer to us than the hospital:
you sound above the factory's ambitious gargle.
Poetry is as useful as a machine!

                     Look at my room.
Guitar strings hold up pictures. I don't need
a piano to sing, and naming things is only the intention
to make things. A locomotive is more melodious
than a cello. I dress in oil cloth and read music
by Guillaume Apollinaire's clay candelabra. Now
my father is dead and has found out you must look things
in the belly, not in the eye. If only he had listened
to the men who made us, hollering like stuck pigs!

LES ÉTIQUETTES JAUNES

I picked up a leaf
today from the sidewalk.
This seems childish.

Leaf! you are so big!
How can you change your
color, then just fall!

As if there were no
such thing as integrity!

You are too relaxed
to answer me. I am too
frightened to insist.

Leaf! don't be neurotic
like the small chameleon.

A PLEASANT THOUGHT FROM WHITEHEAD

Here I am at my desk. The
light is bright enough
to read by it is a warm
friendly day I am feeling
assertive. I slip a few
poems into the pelican's
bill and he is off! out
the window into the blue!

The editor is delighted I
hear his clamor for more
but that is nothing. Ah!
reader! you open the page
my poems stare at you you
stare back, do you not? my
poems speak on the silver
of your eyes your eyes repeat
them to your lover's this
very night. Over your naked
shoulder the improving stars
read my poems and flash
them onward to a friend.

The eyes the poems of the
world are changed! Pelican!
you will read them too!

ANIMALS

Have you forgotten what we were like then
when we were still first rate
and the day came fat with an apple in its mouth

it's no use worrying about Time
but we did have a few tricks up our sleeves
and turned some sharp corners

the whole pasture looked like our meal
we didn't need speedometers
we could manage cocktails out of ice and water

I wouldn't want to be faster
or greener than now if you were with me O you
were the best of all my days

THE THREE-PENNY OPERA

I think a lot about
the Peachums: Polly
and all the rest are
free and fair. Her jewels
have price tags in case
they want to change
hands, and her pets
are carnivorous. Even
the birds.
        Whenever our
splendid hero Mackie
Messer, what an honest
man! steals or kills, there
is meaning for you! Oh
Mackie's knife has a false
handle so it can express
its meaning as well as
his. Mackie's not one to
impose his will. After all
who does own any thing?

But Polly, are you a
shadow? Is Mackie projected
to me by light through film?
If I'd been in Berlin in

1930, would I have seen you
ambling the streets like
Krazy Kat?
           Oh yes. Why,
when Mackie speaks we
only know what he means
occasionally. His sentence
is an image of the times.
You'd have seen all of us
masquerading. Chipper; but
not so well arranged. Air-
ing old poodles and pre-war
furs in narrow shoes
with rhinestone bows.
Silent, heavily perfumed.
Black around the eyes. You
wouldn't have known who
was who, though. Those
were intricate days.

A POEM IN ENVY OF CAVALCANTI

Oh! my heart, although it sounds better
in French, I must say in my native tongue

that I am sick with desire. To be, Guido,
a simple and elegant province all by myself

like you, would mean that a toss of my head,
a wink, a lurch against the nearest brick

had captured painful felicity and all its opaque
nourishment in a near and cosmic stanza, ah!

But I only wither to the earth, my personal
mess, and am unable to utter a good word.

AN IMAGE OF LEDA

The cinema is cruel
like a miracle. We
sit in the darkened
room asking nothing
of the empty white
space but that it
remain pure. And
suddenly despite us
it blackens. Not by
the hand that holds
the pen. There is
no message. We our-
selves appear naked
on the river bank
spread-eagled while
the machine wings
nearer. We scream
chatter prance and
wash our hair! Is
it our prayer or
wish that this
occur? Oh what is

this light that
holds us fast? Our
limbs quicken even
to disgrace under
this white eye as
if there were real
pleasure in loving
a shadow and caress-
ing a disguise!

POEM

Let's take a walk, you
and I in spite of the
weather if it rains hard
                    on our toes

we'll stroll like poodles
and be washed down a
gigantic scenic gutter
                    that will be

exciting! voyages are not
all like this you just put
your toes together then
                    maybe blood

will get meaning and a trick
become slight in our keeping
before we sail the open sea it's
                    possible—

And the landscape will do
us some strange favor when
we look back at each other
                    anxiously

POEM

The ivy is trembling in the hammock
and the air is a brilliant pink
to which I, straddling brilliantly the hummock,
cry "It is today, I think!"

There are white pillars around me
and the grass has stones hidden in it,
my heart is arching over its "Found me?
I'm coming back!" like the eyebrow of a linnet.

O sweet neurosis of a May jump!
pure oar expecting the sea to be white!
it's your stony tear I accept as a slump
in my heart's internationality at night.

O my darling sculpture garden,
you are sorry I went to Alaska?
and if you aren't I am sorrier than a hardon
that refuses to get hard in Alaska.

The sunset is climbing up I think
and I am coming back or going back,
as our love dries itself like ink
after this long swim, this heart attack.

THE ARGONAUTS

The apple green chasuble, so
cut with gold, spins through
the altar like a buzz saw
while nuns melt on the floor.

A skinny Christ, diffident
and extremity relaxed, leans
lightly into the rose window of
the future, and looks away.

The wind squeezes glass leaves,
staining with mulberry the grey
trodden present. Which presently
is scabbed by the sun's healing

cry, not utterly beatific,
yet not the azure exclusion
they had prayed against. Ah!
to be at vespers with Mediterranean

heroes! the muttering drones
casual as surf in our ears,
the black desert which strangles
into adventure our furious host.

THE LOVER

He waits, and it is not without
a great deal of trouble that he tickles
a nightingale with his guitar.

He would like to cry Andiamo!
but alas! no one has arrived
yet although the dew is perfect

for adieux. How bitterly he beats
his hairy chest! because he is
a man, sitting out an indignity.

The mean moon is like a nasty
little lemon above the ubiquitous
snivelling fir trees, and if there's

a swan within a radius of
twelve square miles let's
throttle it. We, too, are worried.

He is a man like us, erect
in the cold dark night. Silence
handles his guitar as clumsily

as a wet pair of dungarees.
The grass is full of snakespit.
He alone is hot amidst the stars.

If no one is racing towards him
down intriguingly hung stairways,
towards the firm lamp of his thighs,

we are indeed in trouble, sprawling
feet upwards to the sun, our faces
growing smaller in the colossal dark.

THE CRITIC

I cannot possibly think of you
other than you are: the assassin

of my orchards. You lurk there
in the shadows, meting out

conversation like Eve's first
confusion between penises and

snakes. Oh be droll, be jolly
and be temperate! Do not

frighten me more than you
have to! I must live forever.

POETRY

The only way to be quiet
is to be quick, so I scare
you clumsily, or surprise
you with a stab. A praying
mantis knows time more
intimately than I and is
more casual. Crickets use
time for accompaniment to
innocent fidgeting. A zebra

races counterclockwise.
All this I desire. To
deepen you by my quickness
and delight as if you
were logical and proven,
but still be quiet as if
I were used to you; as if
you would never leave me
and were the inexorable
product of my own time.

TARQUIN

Exactly at one o'clock your arms broach
the middle of the moon; surf finds its ways
barred by the bold light and a rough loon sways,
bumps in night's ear, a clattering stagecoach.

It is the murmur and the moonstruck ouch!
of love, its glitter in the dark of days
and hurricane of knights' and cowboys' hey!s
on the fragrant plaza, on the hard couch.

The loon resounds like a knock on the door
of the flooded heart, o sweet Roman light
in ribbons over the prairie's collapse!

and the middle of the sea calls on night
to lay her sleeping head upon the shore
and herd the clouds, their mountainous eclipse.

A RANT

"What you wanted I told you"
I said "and what you left me
I took! Don't stand around
my bedroom making things cry

any more! I'm not going to
thrash the floor or throw any
apples! To hell with the radio,
let it rot! I'm not going to be

the monster in my own bed
any more!" Well. The silence
was too easily arrived at; most
oppressive. The pictures swung

on the wall with boredom and
the plants imagined us all in
Trinidad. I was crowded with
windows. I raced to the door.

"Come back" I cried "for a minute!
You left your new shoes. And the
coffee pot's yours!" There were no
footsteps. Wow! what a relief!

INTERIOR (WITH JANE)

The eagerness of objects to
be what we are afraid to do

cannot help but move us   Is
this willingness to be a motive

in us what we reject?   The
really stupid things, I mean

a can of coffee, a 35¢ ear
ring, a handful of hair, what

do these things do to us?   We
come into the room, the windows

are empty, the sun is weak
and slippery on the ice   And a

sob comes, simply because it is
coldest of the things we know

A POSTCARD FROM JOHN ASHBERY

What a message! what a picture!
all pink and gold and classical,
a romantic French sunset for a
change. And the text could not

but inspire—with its hint
of traduction, renaissance, and
Esperanto: verily, The Word! By
what wit do we compound in an
eye "Enée racontant à Didon les
malheurs de la Ville de Troie"
(suburban sexuality and the
milles fleurs that were Rome!)
with "Äneas erzählt Dido das
Missgeschick der Stadt Troya"
(truisms and immer das ewig
Weibliche!) and (garlic oscura,
balliamo! balliamo, my foreign
lover!) "Enea che racconta a
Didone le disgrazie della Città
de Troia" followed by yet an-
other, yet wait! in excess perhaps
but as gleaming as the fandango
that echoes through all of Ravel
"Eneas contando a Dido las desgracias
de la Ciudad de Troya"? (let me
dance! get your hands off me!)
for Guérin was thinking of Moors
and Caramba! flesh is exciting,
even in empirical pictures! No?

A PASTORAL DIALOGUE

The leaves are piled thickly on the green tree
among them squirrels gallop and chuckle

about their emeralds' raindrops; a buckle
like a piece of sun excites them where he

lies drifting in the grass. Towards him they prance,
dart, riot towards the lovers down the mast
and o'er the bounding sod! and she at last
awakes, wakens him quietly. They dance.

"I love you. Their furry eyes and feathers
are for us riches for a shipwrecked pair,
loving on this seashore this forest's porch."

"My hands beneath your skirt don't find weathers,
charts. Should my penis through dangerous air
move up, would you accept it like a torch?"

POEM

I ran through the snow like a young Czarevitch!
My gun was loaded and wolves disguised

as treed nymphs pointed out where the fathers
had hidden in gopher holes. I shot them right

between the eyes! The mothers were harder to find,
they changed themselves into grape arbors, vistas,

and water holes, but I searched for the heart
and shot them there! Then I ran through paper

like a young Czarevitch, strong in the white and cold,
where the shots hung glittering in air like poems.

A SONNET FOR JANE FREILICHER

Wakening at noon I smelled airplanes and hay
rang wildly on long distance telephone
ah! what a misery abed alone
alas! what is that click? hurry! hurray!

the sky was wheeling under sad and grey
sweet clouds but wickedly ne'ertheless shone
outside my lonely coverlets where gone
oh Operator Eighty-one? today

bring me that breath more dear than Fabergé
your secret puissance Operator loan
to pretty Jane whose paintings like a stone

are massive true and silently risqué:
"How closer than Frank to the cosmic bone
comes the bold painting of Fernand Léger"!

A TERRESTRIAL CUCKOO

What a hot day it is! for
Jane and me above the scorch
of sun on jungle waters to be
paddling up and down the Essequibo
in our canoe of war-surplus gondola parts.

We enjoy it, though: the bats squeak
in our wrestling hair, parakeets

bungle lightly into gorges of blossom,
the water's full of gunk and
what you might call waterlilies if you're

silly as we. Our intuitive craft
our striped T shirts and shorts
cry out to vines that are feasting
on flies to make straight the way
of tropical art. "I'd give a lempira or two

to have it all slapped onto a
canvas" says Jane. "How like
lazy flamingos look the floating
weeds! and the infundibuliform
corolla on our right's a harmless Charybdis!

or am I seduced by its ambient
mauve?" The nose of our vessel sneezes
into a bundle of amaryllis, quite
artificially tied with ribbon.
Are there people nearby? and postcards?

We, essentially travellers, frown
and backwater. What will the savages
think if our friends turn up? with
sunglasses and cuneiform decoders!
probably. Oh Jane, is there no more frontier?

We strip off our pretty blazers
of tapa and dive like salamanders
into the vernal stream. Alas! they
have left the jungle aflame, and in
friendly chatter of Kotzebue and Salonika our

friends swiftly retreat downstream
on a flowery float. We strike through
the tongues and tigers hotly, towards
orange mountains, black taboos, dada!
and clouds. To return with absolute treasure!

our only penchant, that. And a red-
billed toucan, pointing t'aurora highlands
and caravanserais of junk, cries out
"New York is everywhere like Paris!
go back when you're rich, behung with lice!"

ON LOOKING AT *LA GRANDE JATTE,*
THE CZAR WEPT ANEW

I

He paces the blue rug. It is the end of summer,
the end of his excursions in the sun. He
may now close his eyes as if they were tired flowers
and feel no sense of duty towards the corridor,
the recherché, the trees; they are all on his face,
a lumpy portrait, a painted desert. He is crying.
Only a few feet away the grass is green, the rug
he sees is grass; and people fetch each other in
and out of shadows there, chuckling and symmetrical.

The sun has left him wide-eyed and alone, hysterical
for snow, the blinding bed, the gun. "Flowers, flowers,
flowers!" he sneers, and echoes fill the spongy trees.
He cannot, after all, walk up the wall. The skylight
is sealed. For why? for a change in the season,
for a refurbishing of the house. He wonders if,
when the music is over, he should not take down
the drapes, take up the rug, and join his friends
out there near the lake, right here beside the lake!
"O friends of my heart!" and they will welcome him
with open umbrellas, fig bars, handmade catapults!
Despite the card that came addressed to someone else,

the sad fisherman of Puvis, despite his own precious
ignorance and the wild temper of the people, he'll try!

2

Now, sitting in the brown satin chair,
he plans a little meal for friends. So!
the steam rising from his Pullman kitchen
fogs up all memories of Seurat, the lake,
the summer; these are over for the moment,
beyond the guests, the cooking sherry and
the gin; such is the palate for sporadic
chitchat and meat. But as the cocktail
warms his courageous cockles he lets
the dinner burn, his eyes widen with
sleet, like a cloudburst fall the summer,
the lake and the voices! He steps into
the mirror, refusing to be anyone else,
and his guests observe the waves break.

3

He must send a telegram from the Ice Palace,
although he knows the muzhiks don't read:
"If I am ever to find these trees meaningful
I must have you by the hand. As it is, they
stretch dusty fingers into an obscure sky,
and the snow looks up like a face dirtied
with tears. Should I cry out and see what happens?
There could only be a stranger wandering
in this landscape, cold, unfortunate, himself
frozen fast in wintry eyes." Explicit Rex.

ANN ARBOR VARIATIONS

1

Wet heat drifts through the afternoon
like a campus dog, a fraternity ghost
waiting to stay home from football games.
The arches are empty clear to the sky.

Except for leaves: those lashes of our
thinking and dreaming and drinking sight.
The spherical radiance, the Old English
look, the sum of our being, "hath perced

to the roote" all our springs and falls
and now rolls over our limpness, a daily
dragon. We lose our health in a love
of color, drown in a fountain of myriads,

as simply as children. It is too hot,
our birth was given up to screaming. Our
life on these street lawns seems silent.
The leaves chatter their comparisons

to the wind and the sky fills up
before we are out of bed. O infinite
our siestas! adobe effigies in a land
that is sick of us and our tanned flesh.

The wind blows towards us particularly
the sobbing of our dear friends on both
coasts. We are sick of living and afraid
that death will not be by water, o sea.

2

Along the walks and shaded ways
pregnant women look snidely at children.
Two weeks ago they were told, in these

selfsame pools of trefoil, "the market
for emeralds is collapsing," "chlorophyll
shines in your eyes," "the sea's misery

is progenitor of the dark moss which hides
on the north side of trees and cries."
What do they think of slim kids now?

and how, when the summer's gong of day
and night slithers towards their sweat
and towards the nests of their arms

and thighs, do they feel about children
whose hides are pearly with days of swimming?
Do they mistake these fresh drops for tears?

The wind works over these women constantly!
trying, perhaps, to curdle their milk
or make their spring unseasonably fearful,

season they face with dread and bright eyes.
The leaves, wrinkled or shiny like apples,
wave women courage and sigh, a void temperature.

3
The alternatives of summer do not remove
us from this place. The fainting into skies
from a diving board, the express train to
Detroit's damp bars, the excess of affection
on the couch near an open window or a Bauhaus
fire escape, the lazy regions of stars, all
are strangers. Like Mayakovsky read on steps
of cool marble, or Yeats danced in a theatre
of polite music. The classroom day of dozing
and grammar, the partial eclipse of the head
in the row in front of the head of poplars,
sweet Syrinx! last out the summer in a stay
of iron. Workmen loiter before urinals, stare

out windows at girders tightly strapped to clouds.
And in the morning we whimper as we cook
an egg, so far from fluttering sands and azure!

4
The violent No! of the sun
burns the forehead of hills.
Sand fleas arrive from Salt Lake
and most of the theatres close.

The leaves roll into cigars, or
it seems our eyes stick together
in sleep. O forest, o brook of
spice, o cool gaze of strangers!

the city tumbles towards autumn
in a convulsion of tourists
and teachers. We dance in the dark,
forget the anger of what we blame

on the day. Children toss and murmur
as a rumba blankets their trees and
beckons their stars closer, older, now.
We move o'er the world, being so much here.

It's as if Poseidon left off counting
his waters for a moment! In the fields
the silence is music like the moon.
The bullfrogs sleep in their hairy caves,

across the avenue a trefoil lamp
of the streets tosses luckily.
The leaves, finally, love us! and
moonrise! we die upon the sun.

A MEXICAN GUITAR

Actors with their variety of voices
and nuns, those arch campaign-managers,
were pacing the campo in contrasting colors
as Jane and I muttered a red fandango.

A cloud flung Jane's skirt in my face
and the neighborhood boys saw such sights
as mortal eyes are usually denied. Arabian day!
she clicked her rhinestone heels! vistas of lace!

Our shouting knocked over a couple of palm trees
and the gaping sky seemed to reel at our mistakes,
such purple flashing insteps and careers!
which bit with lavish envy the northern soldiers.

Then loud startling deliberation! Violet peered,
hung with silver trinkets, from an adobe slit,
escorted by a famished movie star, beau idéal!
crooning that dejected ballad, "Anne the Strip."

"Give me back my mink!" our Violet cried
"and cut out the heroics! I'm from Boston, remember."
Jane and I plotz! what a mysteriosabelle!
the fandango died on our lips, a wintry fan.

And all that evening eating peanut paste and onions
we chattered, sad, of films and the film industry
and how ballet is dying. And our feet ached. Violet
burst into tears first, she is always in the nick of time.

JANE AWAKE

The opals hiding in your lids
    as you sleep, as you ride ponies
mysteriously, spring to bloom
    like the blue flowers of autumn

each nine o'clock. And curls
    tumble languorously towards
the yawning rubber band, tan,
    your hand pressing all that

riotous black sleep into
    the quiet form of daylight
and its sunny disregard for
    the luminous volutions, oh!

and the budding waltzes
    we swoop through in nights.
Before dawn you roar with
    your eyes shut, unsmiling,

your volcanic flesh hides
    everything from the watchman,
and the tendrils of dreams
    strangle policemen running by

too slowly to escape you,
    the racing vertiginous waves
of your murmuring need. But
    he is day's guardian saint

that policeman, and leaning
    from your open window you ask
him what dress to wear and how
    to comb your hair modestly,

for that is now your mode.
    Only by chance tripping on stairs
do you repeat the dance, and
      then, in the perfect variety of

subdued, impeccably disguisèd,
    white black pink blue saffron
and golden ambiance, do we find
      the nightly savage, in a trance.

1951

Alone at night
in the wet city

the country's wit
is not memorable.

The wind has blown
all the trees down

but these anxieties
remain erect, being

the heart's deliberate
chambers of hurt

and fear whether
from a green apartment

seeming diamonds or
from an airliner

seeming fields. It's
not simple or tidy

though in rows of
rows and numbered;

the literal drifts
colorfully and

the hair is combed
with bridges, all

compromises leap
to stardom and lights.

If alone I am
able to love it,

the serious voices,
the panic of jobs,

it is sweet to me.
Far from burgeoning

verdure, the hard way
is this street.

ASHES ON SATURDAY AFTERNOON

The banal machines are exposing themselves
on nearby hillocks of arrested color: why

if we are the anthropologist's canapé
should this upset the autumn afternoon?

It is because you are silent. Speak, if
speech is not embarrassed by your attention
to the scenery! in languages more livid than
vomit on Sunday after wafer and prayer.

What is the poet for, if not to scream
himself into a hernia of admiration for all
paradoxical integuments: the kiss, the
bomb, cathedrals and the zeppelin anchored

to the hill of dreams? Oh be not silent
on this distressing holiday whose week
has been a chute of sand down which no
factories or castles tumbled: only my

petulant two-fisted heart. You, dear poet,
who addressed yourself to flowers, Electra,
and photographs on less painful occasions,
must save me from the void's external noise.

COMMERCIAL VARIATIONS

I
"When you're ready to sell your diamonds
it's time to go to the Empire State Building"
and jump into the 30s like they did in 1929.
Those were desperate days too, but I'd no more
give up our silver mine, Belle, just because gold
has become the world standard look, than all

your grey hairs, beloved New York from whence
all the loathsome sirens don't call. They would like
to take you away from me wouldn't they? now that the fever's
got me and there're rumors of a Rush in California
and pine fields in Massachusetts as yet unindustrialized.
That's how they act to The American Boy
from Sodom-on-Hudson (non-resident membership
in The Museum of Modern Art) as if it weren't the best
little municipality in the U.S. with real estate
rising like a coloratura, no road sighs, and self-plumbing;
and more damned vistas of tundra than Tivoli
has dolce far niente. It's me, though, not the city—
oh my god don't let them take me away! wire *The Times.*

2

Last year I entertained I practically serenaded
Zinka Milanov when the Metropolitan Opera Company
(and they know a good thing) came to S-on-H, and now
I'm expected to spend the rest of my days in a north-state
greenhouse where the inhabitants don't even know
that the "Jewel Song"'s from *Carmen.* They think oy
is short for oysters. I may be tough and selfish, but
what do you expect? my favorite play is *William Tell.*
You can't tell me the city's wicked: I'm wicked.
The difference between your climate and mine is
that up north in the Aurora Borealis the blame falls like rain.
In the city's mouth if you're hit in the eye it's the sun
or a fist, no bushing around the truth, whatever that is.
I like it when the days are ducal and you worry fearlessly.
Minding the Governor your lover, and the witch your sister,
how they thought of the least common denominator and're dazzling!

3

The sky has opened like a solarium and the artillery
of the pest has peddled into the feathery suffering
its recently published rhymes. How that lavender weeping
and beastly curses would like to claim the soldiers its own,

and turn the "tide" of the war! But they, shining,
mush back to The Trojan Horse, climb up, and ride away.

4
Yes, the mathematicians applauded when the senator
proved that god never sent cablegrams or disappeared
except when voodoo or political expediency flourished,
it being sweet times, in Tammany in the 90s
and before one hated to seem too cocky or too ritzy.
One thought a good deal then of riding for pleasures
and in shrubbery of a casual fistfight Vesuvius smarting
and screaming creamed rubily as if to flush the heavens.
As the glassy fencing of sunrise in a fish market
cries out its Americanism and jingoes and jolts daily
over the icebergs of our historically wispy possum-drowsy
lack of antiquity, we know that art must be vulgar to say
"Never may the dame claim to be warm to the exact,
nor the suburban community amount to anything in any way
that is not a pursuit of the purple vices artsy-craftsy,
the loom in the sitting room where reading is only aloud
and illustrative of campfire meetings beside the Out Doors
where everyone feels as ill at ease as sea-food."

Often I think of your voice against the needles of dawn
when the dampness was operatic in Ann Arbor lilacs
and the gold of my flesh had yet to be regimented in freckles.
Now I must face the glass of whatever sliver's my smile,
each day more demanding me for what I have always tossed aside
like listening to *Erwartung* hanging by your thumbs;
I turn grey over night screaming feverishly scoreful, note
for note as I have always believed, for I know what I love
and know what must be trodden under foot to be vindicated
and glorified and praised: Belle of Old New York
your desperation will never open in *La Forza del Destino*
which was my father's favorite opera when he tried to jump
out a window on New Year's Eve in 1940, thirty days
before I ditched the stable boy who gave me the diamonds
I'm turning in today for a little freedom to travel.

COLLOQUE SENTIMENTAL

"It's too wrestling at the beach the sand
the sand shackles the wrists shunt."

Tired and walking's slighter than grips eye.
"The big book for dinner and after, gin.

I want you to succeed but strap you
beauty befuddled and its soothing filth?"

Grass on the screens and those mosquitoes
humming humming. "Gee I don't know

if bawling really interests me. When I was
Scandinavia sang two days but I three away

all the money." The wind's cold plunging
apart strides into narrow staring caves.

"I love you more than life itself, but what's
most painful is most peaceful and I

I must be punished because I'm popular.
It's wet and your neck is knotted with mine."

DAY AND NIGHT IN 1952

Be not obedient of the excellent, do not prize the silly with an exceptionally
pushy person or orphan. The ancient world knew these things and I am unable
to convey as well as those poets the simplicity of things, the bland and amused

stare of garages and banks, the hysterical bark of a dying dog which is not unconcerned with human affairs but dwells in the cave of the essential passivity of his kind. Kine? their warm sweet breaths exist nowhere but in classical metre, bellowing and puling throughout the ages of our cognizance like roses in romances. We do not know any more the exquisite manliness of all brutal acts because we are sissies and if we're not sissies we're unhappy and too busy. Be not discouraged by your own inept affection. I don't want any of you to be really unhappy, just camp it up a bit and whine, whineola, baby. I'm talking to you over there, isn't this damn thing working? You're just the one I'm talking to. Don't you understand what's going on around here? It's not that I want you to be so knowing as all that, but I don't want some responsibility to be shown in the modern world's modernity, your face and mine dashing across the steppes of a country which is only partially occupied and acceptable, and is very windy and grassy and rugged. I speak of New Jersey, of course, the always acceptable and dismal, a farewell view of which might knock you right on your nose, poor sentimental dear that I know you are. What do you want of me? or my friends? or all the dopes you make demands of in toilets, there's no gratuity for you in it. Accept that, my bright turgid little tamarind. Are you still listening, cutie? you who dresses in pumps for the routine, shorts, a tuxedo jacket and a sequin tophat? you are delicious I don't mind letting you know. If we were some sort of friends I might have to bitch you; as it is you can have whatever you want from anyone else and whatever somewhat in-accurate cooperation you may care to have from me. I'm not this way with people I know. And they're not with me. John, for instance, thinks I am the child of my own old age; Jimmy is cagey with snide remarks while he washes dishes and I pose in the bathroom; Jane is rescuing herself at the mercy of her ill temper towards me which is expressed only in the riddles of her motival phantasies; what am I to say of Larry? who really resents the fact that I may be conning him instead of Vice and Art; Grace may secretly distrust me but we are both so close to the abyss that we must see a lot of each other, grinning and carrying on as if it were a picnic given by somebody else's church; Kenneth continually goes away and by this device is able to remain intensely friendly if not actually intimate; but the other John catches everyone of my innuendi the wrong way or at the very least obliquely and is never mistaken or ill-tempered, which is what I worry about the most. What can I do? I can

and then I, ravished and indeed under an enormous pressure of circumstance, paced the carpet, opened the casement, plunged my perspiring hands into a basin of iced cologne my mother had thoughtfully left in a corner on a large teatable, wrinkled and unwrinkled my brow in a ripple of anxiety, and felt desperately ill. The window opened on a broad lawn and behind, as if accidentally, a vista of dunes which were incredibly boring and strange. Do you occasionally wonder at the inscrutable nature of visual experiences, an undeniable and far from optometrical

distance? the bane and bolster of
my primping prissy heart's bane of
anguish! the pressure wheel stone of
desire. I do not want to be victim of
the ability to enthuse myself at or of
and especially kissy people who are of
the darker race. Did I say Dark? of
what comparative device may I avail myself of
pretending to be the Queen of Africa and of
Suez. Perhaps more especially of
Suez, since Aden is most beautiful of
courses, having the famous flamingoes of
Saratoga flown over for that weekend of
mad irregular what else! Of
distances I can only say Paris! you of
the paper route, you fictitious of
all the prancers in my ardent imagination of
which are you not the least and most of
what I think about the world of
no illusion, not an iota! Not hated of
my shuddering pressure and ending, of
my interminable self-disciplines, of
the symbol which is the lover not of
the people who neither care nor of
pleasaunces are chary, an apple-headed putsch of
Vienna and those light-skinned pusses. So of
you I am least proud in mind and most of
my thoughts are blue with miles of
figures and chariots and nudes on paths of
primrose, going down the drain of
modern times like a rhymed heroic tragedienne of
patsies and opening nights and visions of
the madame who cares and knows not what of.

EASTER

The razzle dazzle maggots are summary
tattooing my simplicity on the pitiable.
The perforated mountains of my saliva leave cities awash
more exclusively open and more pale than skirts.
O the glassy towns are fucked by yaks
slowly bleeding a quiet filigree on the leaves of that souvenir
of a bird chastely crossing the boulevard of falling stars
cold in the dull heavens
drowned in flesh,
it's the night like I love it all cruisy and nelly
fingered fan of boskage fronds the white smile of sleeps.

When the world strips down and rouges up
like a mattress's teeth brushed by love's bristling sun
a marvellous heart tiresomely got up in brisk bold stares
when those trappings fart at the feet of the stars
a self-coral serpent wrapped round an arm with no jujubes
without swish
without camp
floods of crocodile piss and pleasures of driving
shadows of prairie pricks dancing
of the roses of Pennsylvania looking in eyes noses and ears
those windows at the head of science.
I supplicate
dirty blonde mermaids leaning on their elbows
rigor mortis sculpting the figure of those iron tears,
all the feathers falling font a sea of yuccas and blue riddles
every Nevada fantastic has lost his dolorous teeth
when the world, smutty abstract, powders its pearls
the gardens of the sea's come
a mast of the barcantine lost flaming bearer of hurricanes
a hardon a sequoia a toilet tissue
a reject of poor people
in squeezing your deflowered eyeballs

all the powdered and pomaded balloon passengers
voluntarily burning their orifices to a cinder
a short circuit in the cow eyes' sour milk
eyes sucked by fever
the x-ray night's mercury prophylaxis
women who use cigars
the sea swallowing tumultuous islands
is burnt by the sun like a girl
a sieve of stinking villages
a muff of mosquitoes in the walking dark
pouring demented chinchillas
trumpets fell, many the virulent drapery lids
the murdered raining softly on yellow oranges
violating the opaque sexual privileges of twilight
the big nigger of noon
just as the floor of the ocean crushes pebbles
too eager for the appetites of little feet.

Giving and getting the pubic foliage of precarious hazard
sailors
Silent ripples in a bayou of raffish bumpkin winks
sweet meat packers touting the herb bracelets of pus
kisses! kisses!
fresher than the river that runs like a moon through girls.
And the swamped ship flouncing to the portholes at the eagle hour
earrings

the ship sawed up by the biting asses of stars
at the heaving buttocks of coupling drydocks
and the ship latches onto a sideboard of sourdough
sends telegrams by camel and dodo
an aloof dancer practicing push-ups on top of the mast
all night you see them plunging and swizzling
pouncing elegantly in that jewelled grass
an army of frigates
an army of cocks
an army of wounds
an army of young married couples' vanilla hemorrhages

a spine-tingling detonation nested in leaves
alfalfa blowing against sisters in a hanky of shade
and the tea ship crushes an army of hair
in rampant jaws those streets whose officer deploys a day of
hairs strutting the rosy municipal ruts
hairs brushing the seaflowers and tapestries from the gums
of the shore

birdie, birdie
on the uptown train
dining in the midst of waiters
O the bread of colleens butters the rain.
A minute more and earth would grab the crater's lip
and a wind of diamonds rough up red sultans
and their cast off whores, chemises!
shuffling their shoes to a milky number about sugar
in the gardens of the rainbow planted by anarchists
whose hairy sheets cover the nits of canaries
brushed out by henna specialists.
When the world has walked the tightrope that ties up our eyes
when the world has stretched the rubber skin of sleep
when the world is just a cluttered box for your cluttered box
and charges through the cream of your smiling entrails
like a Pope
sounding box of tomorrow champion box alarm
at the call of mystics and pilots
box raining sadly over Sicily and over the bars
and the weekly tooth brush

furious senses your lianas forest the virgin
O sins of sex and kisses of birds at the end of the penis
cry of a black princess whose mouth founders in the Sun
a million gardens fill the white furry sky
black pillow cast on the retreating flood of night
absurd ice under the hand's breast of dark
bitten by smiles habitual, the giggle
in the blue lidded eyes of prunes
a dawn of justice and magnetic mines

the princess in the clear heart of summer sucks her flower
and honey drowns her in a green valley
she is privately caught in the breeze blown silence
night without eyelids
tied to the jet of my mysterious galley
my cuckoo my boomerang
I have sunk my tongue in the desperation of her blood
strangely her features are Easter
and the balm of Easter floods, my tongue's host
a rivulet of purple blood runs over the wise hands
of sobbing infants.
And the ship shoves off into the heady oceans of love
whose limpidity is the exile of the self
I cry the moon to shower fishes and tears over her
runners through the warring surf of Red Indians
on the California shore, that nausea
not swamp the wind's hand of the Sun
towering afire over the living islands and hairy waves
not forgotten in the silken sound of fruits
proud shout the coyotes and the orchids of the testicles.

Boom of pregnant hillsides
awash with urine
a tambourine relieving the earth beside a hedge
when the fingers tap against the spine it's cherry time
where are the suburbs of powdered corpses dancing
O the amusing audience to all words shivers
before the flashing sword of the thighs of the Sun
like a hangar the sun fries all mumbojumboes
and the rivers scramble like lizards about the ankle
until the ravishing pronunciamento of stone.

Black bastard black prick black pirate whose cheek
batters the heavenly heart
and signs its purple in the ribs of nightly explosion
Sun boom
sleep trooped about by paid assassins mad for kisses
from the bamboo bottle of the Father of Heaven, race

whom I quit as the salamander quits the flame.
The day passes into the powdery light of your embrace
like an Alaskan desert over the basket of Mexico
before the coming of the Spics. River rushing into the Sun
to become golden and drossy drip the fingernails
the molluscs on the underside of the scrotum
embroidered with lice and saliva and berries
the Sun sings in the stones of the savage
when the world booms its seven cunts
like a river plunged upon and perishing
Sun, to the feast!
to be pelted by the shit of the stars at last in flood
like a breath.

CHEZ JANE

The white chocolate jar full of petals
swills odds and ends around in a dizzying eye
of four o'clocks now and to come. The tiger,
marvellously striped and irritable, leaps
on the table and without disturbing a hair
of the flowers' breathless attention, pisses
into the pot, right down its delicate spout.
A whisper of steam goes up from that porcelain
urethra. "Saint-Saëns!" it seems to be whispering,
curling unerringly around the furry nuts
of the terrible puss, who is mentally flexing.
Ah be with me always, spirit of noisy
contemplation in the studio, the Garden
of Zoos, the eternally fixed afternoons!
There, while music scratches its scrofulous

stomach, the brute beast emerges and stands,
clear and careful, knowing always the exact peril
at this moment caressing his fangs with
a tongue given wholly to luxurious usages;
which only a moment before dropped aspirin
in this sunset of roses, and now throws a chair
in the air to aggravate the truly menacing.

BLOCKS

1

Yippee! she is shooting in the harbor! he is jumping
up to the maelstrom! she is leaning over the giant's
cart of tears which like a lava cone let fall to fly
from the cross-eyed tantrum-tousled ninth grader's
splayed fist is freezing on the cement! he is throwing
up his arms in heavenly desperation, spacious Y of his
tumultuous love-nerves flailing like a poinsettia in
its own nailish storm against the glass door of the
cumulus which is withholding her from these divine
pastures she has filled with the flesh of men as stones!
O fatal eagerness!

2

O boy, their childhood was like so many oatmeal cookies.
I need you, you need me, yum, yum. Anon it became suddenly

3

like someone always losing something and never knowing what.
Always so. They were so fond of eating bread and butter and
sugar, they were slobs, the mice used to lick the floorboards
after they went to bed, rolling their light tails against

the rattling marbles of granulation. Vivo! the dextrose
those children consumed, lavished, smoked, in their knobby
candy bars. Such pimples! such hardons! such moody loves.
And thus they grew like giggling fir trees.

ALMA

"Est-elle almée? . . . aux premières heures bleues
Se détruira-t-elle comme les fleurs feues. . . ."
                                    —*Rimbaud*

I

The sun, perhaps three of them, one black one red, you know, and her dancing
all the time, fanning the purple sky getting purple, her fancy white skin quite
unoriental to the dirty children's round eyes standing in circles munching muf-
fins, the cockroaches like nuggets half hid in the bran. Boy! how are you,
Prester John? the smile of the river, so searching, so enamelled.

2

What mention of the King?
the spinning wheel still turns,
the apples rot to the singing,
Alceste on winter sojourns

is nice at Nice. Wander,
my dear sacred Pontiff, do dare
to murder minutely and ponder
what is the bloody affair

inside the heart of the weak
dancer, whose one toe is worth
inestimable, the gang, the cheek
of it! it's too dear, her birth

amidst the acorns with nails
stuck through them by passionate
parents, castanets! Caucasian tales!
their prodigality proportionate:

"Sacred Heart, oh Heart so sick,
make Detroit more wholly thine,
all with greeds and scabs so thick
that Judas Priest must make a sign."

Thus he to bed and we to rise
and Alma singing like a loon.
Her dancing toenails in her eyes.
Her pa was dead on the River Gaboon.

3

Detroit was founded on the great near waterways next to Canada which was friendly and immediately gained for herself the appellation "the Detroit of Thermopylaes," a name which has stuck to this day wherever ballroom dancing is held in proper esteem. Let me remind you of that great wrist movement, the enjambement schizophrene, a particularly satisfying variation of which may be made by adding a little tomato paste. Great success. While in Detroit accused of starting the Chicago fire. Millions of roses from Russians. Alma had come a long way, she opened a jewelry shop, her name became a household word, she'd invented an arch-supporter.

How often she thought of her father! the castle, the kitchen-garden, the hollihocks and the mill stream beyond curving gently as a parenthesis. Many a bitter tear was shed by her on the boards of this theatre as she pondered the inscrutable meagerness of divine Providence, always humming, always shifting a little, never missing a beat. She guested one season at the height of her nostalgia with the Metropolitan Opera Ballet in *Salammbô;* her father seemed very close in all that oriental splendor of bamboo and hotel palms and stale sweat and bracelets, an engagement of tears. In the snow, in her white fox fur wraps, how more beautiful than Mary Garden!

4

Onward to the West. "Where I came from,
where I'm going. Indian country." Gold.

Oh say can you see Alma. The darling
of Them. All her friends were artists.
They alone have memories. They alone
love flowers. They alone give parties
and die. Poor Alma. They alone.
                                    She died,
and it was as if all the jewels in the world
had heaved a sigh. The seismograph
at Fordham University registered, for once,
a spiritual note. How like a sliver
in her own short fat muscular foot.
She loved the Western World, though
there are some who say she isn't really dead.

HATRED

I have a terrible age and I part
my name at the seams of the beast
in a country of robbers who prepare meals
for a velvet church green with stammerers
and with cuckoos, with cormorants and cranes.

I've tucked the rushing earth under my legs
so I won't have to turn my back on Sundays
and the morasses of ritual archers milking,
and I eat in a prison of bread and mortar,
I eat the stuff with the wooden provocations.

But if I'd broken you one of my wings,
shaft darkening over the prairie of your soul,
for the sea's split resistance I'd never snout.

I'd retch up all men. I would give
up America and her twenty twistings of my years.

The footsteps and suspirations of a twig!
and these given me by ransom. America
watches at the feet of my ramparting brow
and in a three thousand of years of brutes
will violate the wistful sphinx of myself

beneath an arch, latched onto poles
like the doors of comrades forced wide open
to the lost wind of a night on its back
supping whatever free entrails. Hounds,
the drab chefs, the menacing drones and icemen

who whirl towards us with bleakest confidence,
I have hounded myself out of the coral mountains
when my flesh quivered controllably upwards
into the chimneys of a black horde
which were the liberty to work beautifully.

I hounded and hounded into being born
my own death and the death of my country
at the stick, aloft and articulate,
so that the wry words of prophetic ravens
recognized themselves in clutching my wounds

and instantly died as I have wished to be dead
lately. For the delivery of the ensign
upon the painless body which is an island
I alone accept the blue breath of princes, for I
have done it. Am General and Ghost.

I have prized those days most dolefully
which saw me able to disrobe in the savage foam
of spears not polished to celebrate marriages.
I have never feared to suck out the soldier's brag
and so return to cadavers resuscitated on other shores

where war and its raptures is the only light,
and more dire than sisters. I don't wish to tear
the Chinese or their dogs into an intellectual smile,
nor does catching the ripe gules of enemy crossfire
upon my eyelashes signify Life in Death to me,

not when the corpses still circle my sweating front
like laurel. There are millions who'd like to see
that they meet the elderly dead in noisy churches
throughout a land that famine wooed garretless:
for these I paint the signs of the rounds of the latrines.

Two by two. They love Force while still hooked
otherward like two flies in a breeze, but let that other
pace the sheep and incense of a streetcorner on night
and they all go down, beneath dust-flower quilts
where the chosen homeland sweats and feels no winds.

But the war. How shall it claw me up?
and rip America sideways into pieces and shreds of blood.
The warriors clash into their ginlike fusillades
and are asleep before any thin arms entwine them,
having betrayed the numbers but never blabbed.

All! I cry who am all
where the plain bee on my body farms out gold,
do not wish my brittle bones to be dough on the tooth
held like a cleft palate in a bus of silver
by lame emigrants who do not love to go further.

I have resisted my comrades and their parties.
The general reunion called "Kindertoten" and "Jadis"
I'd use as a bomb to salve the voters who read
that youth, that age must rest on the divine.
But where is the first acrobat, and a woman kneeling?

Parting, the sugar in my breast that's fatuous
in moving and in pushing on, who'll shout a name

where mankind is no longer drowning? Hatred itself
can find no railroads into that sublime country
and slavery will not just burst like a volcano.

Yet I hold myself to you. I have the jangling nerves
of legendary people who box each other's ears and if
it is a union of saxophones and harps and heroes
in me you may discover the gossamer draperies
of defecation and death, and a love for the ancient kings.

What delight tricks you into stripping down
like lousy children who give away their few books
avariciously, and find that all their friends are blind?
I am afraid your kisses, so bland, lean against garages
and are worn out in the white nights of superintendents.

The arrest of the poor struggles into posters
and I bleed through a pose of cautious elephant riding,
am caught in brambles fancy as myself as prisoner
of Chillon. It is against this self that I hasten
towards a higher malady in which you appear starred

as aspiration and regret. The world's years
of war turn like walls of bottles and strangled soldiers
in my breast. I speak òf liberty as if a girl
had just been eaten by our tribe between two lumps
of flaming coal, sacrifice to the foibles of cannon.

They have shot up the Just and shunted them
past the falls up to the daisied cliff-dwellers
where I merit, against my will, the careerism of
an Apache. Those compromises in the form of a cross
blot from my face the bony verdure of the clouds

and with a vicarious red salute trailing away
into the image in snot of Christ I refrain
from the maize and the manly savors and tongues
that cry hollowing "Aurora" as I fall upon rocks,
hearing always the churches sinking onto the bored earth.

Herons and priests who do not wear guns or skirts
and who infiltrate drunkenly the pillows and barricades
of what were condemned as castles, how may oppression
strongly enough refuse to resign itself to breathing
the silence of the open air and the praised and the careless?

I have been hunted in the purple arms of a lover
whose twilight had been commanded me for the people's sake,
how ridiculous! and they hurled those first stones
which turned our sobs to plums and sank my head
upon the brown flower which is at once Sun and Eagle.

No revolutionary canticle broke the mist
of that casque, and somewhere like a starry curtain
we drifted towards the Outer, where new myths
lay gasping at our white vanquished languor.
As martyr I am able to whip the crowd into shape,

a coronet of renegades dangling gold in the sky
like fountains and arenas on which feasts the cruel azure
of the holiday immediately succeeding the comradeship
of battle, and the endless chants of fishermen
who are heavy with seining for pyramids and swallows

and find the destroyer like a palace in a nightmare
about anarchists. I shall forget forever America,
which was like a memory of an island massacre
in the black robes of my youthful fear of shadows.
So easily conquered by the black torrent of this knife.

INVINCIBILITY

"In the church of my heart the choir is on fire!"
                  —Vladimir Mayakovsky

I

Avarice, the noose that lets oil, oh my dear oh
"La Ronde," erase what is assured and ours, it
resurrects nothing, finally, in its eagerness
to sit under the widely spaced stairs, to be a fabulous
toilette, doesn't imitate footsteps of disappearance

The neighbor, having teased peace to retire, soon
averages six flowering fountains, ooh! spare the men
and their nervous companions that melt and ripen
into a sordid harbor of squid-slipping tarpaulin strips,
quits the sordid arbor of community butchers' girth

The jumping error pins hate on the blossoms of baffles,
densely foraging covered hero–Nero of Maltese, of Moor,
leap, oh leap! against the fame that's in the noose,
sister of yearning, of eclogues without overcoats deeply,
and the trumpet rages over the filigreed prisoners

Now sallies forth the joyousness of being cruel
which is singing of the world needed by the paralyzed wind,
seated and rebeginning, mounting without saying adieu,
never again delicately to entomb a tear,
that mark of suffering in the toughness of the forest

Lepers nest on the surly cats of glistening delirium,
feet of fire drowning in the attitude of relinquishing foreheads
remember always the barriers so cupiditously defended,
no spume breezy enough for the tempestuous sabers
sent reeling into the charades of fears of the nubile

A crisis questions its attendant in the eyelid of Verona
so serious are the lassitudes of a heart turned into a choir
and the fire-escapes tend to ferment against the paynim cheek
of love that's advancing into a maelstrom for a true speech,

succoring the lewd paupers deliberately, spearlike,
the pearl hesitating to come near the arid well

Noose arriving tropically masterful, estimating and caught,
let the crouching ferns release their nascent sonata
and, shaking with a remuneration of flaccid countries,
eat the rum that cruises an immortally non-sequitur finish,
quaint, and having an aspiration as of torrents and cars

Touched by the insensitivity that broods over the boats,
oh halos of startling carpets, canoes and lathes! archers!
a January of feeling seats itself before the young soldiers
and laughs and laughs at those arch-guardians' radiance,
particularly the sneer of fate, habit shaking its white fists

2
Now for some hell, you make a few fast purchases
separated by first nights of yoyo-cartwheel-violences,
ill but yelling and running full of the younger luminosity,
soulful, oh and epic and sort of rouged between the shoulder blades!
which the striding has not succeeded in making a gondola yet
and this has so devastated the murmuring contributions of strangers
in suits under the brilliant heather, although, my soul! it's white
it's painted white as the rain! and have you not taught for clarity,
for that sweet sake, the worldly dream of the son marching outward
always? and whispering of sins in the green clouds

An eagerness for the historical look of the mirror,
the dry smile of knowledge which is faithlessness apologizing
to the Sphinx, and is it not a great fury of horsemen
who make a guided tour of the future and its glasslike tortures?
the odor of evening vibrating across that linear nostalgia
and vouchsafing a plume and a volume of Plato,
purblind water, the earth pitting its stench against the moon's
and accomplishing a serenade, a terrestrial touchdown sigh
in the silence which is not yet formidable or ominous,
resenting the leaves and not yet geared to the undercutting foam

SAVOY

It's cutting into me on its bareback with talons lifted
like a bespectacled carapaceous witch doctor of Rimini
beautifying an adolescent tubbed in entrails of blue cement
rattling his bells and fox tails and teeth in hydrogen peroxide
under a velour hammock swinging to the bubbles of traffic
of silver striated poppy seeds, milky buses ending in screams
their pods! and a hot wind boring into the cellars of sentiment
which is no more than the animal world, isn't it architectural?
panting its appreciation. You are too late, you are violent,
everyone will know how the man furrows his wet beak,
my nerves will get to the air, and more involved in themselves
than an acanthus issue a somewhat sluggish declaration of wah-wah.
They're calling up the drums to find out if my mask has
buffeted sacks of Congo grass to hide my soul. Great bones
of my knees lifting me hillward! who are you?

O loud timber leg of ore listening to the abutting hoots
and the compensatory descriptions of tin in the banks!
The flour and the fuel of white drill presses is ending!
envelops the corvette which is riddling the farming pillow
diving upon the mustang whose whiskers thump their master,
O great soulful scandal in the courtyard of clairvoyance!
O comatose lips of charcoal going down on the horizon!
the barrages are zooming over the pretty flotillas and bandannas.

Doubtful vendors of stick-seats in the doorway of the furnace,
O doubtful verifiers of the quality of cerise-streaked pus
lying luminously obliterated and sure on a circus salary,
knell of the appealing Wednesday rallying against vices,
knell of sobbing fairies retenting their nut farms and moors,
your fenestrations are full of snow!
O coupling of strangers in the longings of grease!
Evoi!
Dropping warriors champing at their derailed perils

down to the main stream of the never engulfed fund of mares,
tough, serious, consummated, tough, serious, pardoned,
pain willfully enfranchising the foreskin and new wizardry
and puking a little into the jar, pulsating as new ambergris,
do you tender the bounty which has availed itself of your pride?

WALKING TO WORK

It's going to be the sunny side
from now
            on. Get out, all of you.

This is my traffic over the night
and how
            should I range my pride

each oceanic morning like a cutter
if I
      confuse the dark world is round
round who
            in my eyes at morning saves

nothing from nobody? I'm becoming
the street.
            Who are you in love with?
me?
      Straight against the light I cross.

SECOND AVENUE

In memory of Vladimir Mayakovsky

I

Quips and players, seeming to vend astringency off-hours,
celebrate diced excesses and sardonics, mixing pleasures,
as if proximity were staring at the margin of a plea . . .

This thoroughness whose traditions have become so reflective,
your distinction is merely a quill at the bottom of the sea
tracing forever the fabulous alarms of the mute
so that in the limpid tosses of your violet dinginess
a pus appears and lingers like a groan from the collar
of a reproachful tree whose needles are tired of howling.
One distinguishes merely the newspapers of a sediment,
since going underground is like discovering something in
your navel that has an odor and is able to fly away.
I must bitterly reassure the resurgence of your complaints
for you, like all heretics, penetrate my glacial immodesty,
and I am a nun trembling before the microphone
at a movie première while a tidal wave has seized the theatre
and borne it to Siam, decorated it and wrecked its projector.
To what leaf of fertility and double-facedness owe I
my persistent adoration of your islands, oh shadowed flesh
of my smiling? I scintillate like a glass of ice
and it is all for you and the boa constrictors who entertain
your doubts with a scarf dance called "Bronx Tambourine."
Grappling with images of toothpaste falling on guitar strings,
your lips are indeed a disaster of alienated star-knots
as I deign to load the hips of the swimming pool, lumber!
with the clattering caporal of destiny's breast-full,
such exhalations and filthiness falling upon the vegetables!
You will say I am supernatural.
Varying your task with immortal plunging justices and fruits,
I suffer accelerations that are vicarious and serene,
just as the lances of an army advance above the heat of the soldiery,
so does my *I* tremble before the getting-out-of-bedness
of that all-encompassing snake warned-off in pocket-books

as "him," and subtitled elsewhere "couch," "marvel," "ears,"
or "fire-escape," "lampooned frigid scalper of an Amazon maid,"
"warrior of either sex in the distances which are American";
and just as it is a miracle to find her in the interrogation
of an escalator, you find yourself racing towards nervousness,
the purée of crime, and your face has fallen like a waffle
and is the velour of Lesbian sandals with nails in the toes;
your lamp will never light without dirt and the speed
increases of moving away from all rapturous ice-floes
as a shaggy white figure approaches and sinks its fangs
upon my brazen throat, so thrust into the wind that a necklace
of fur such as this which drags me beneath the Bering Sea
is the only possible adornment for this burning flight
and the magnificent entrance to be mine as I crash
against the portals of the mistress of chairs, who is
yes, a bearded man suspended by telephone wires from moons
in alternate sexual systems. And then there is the crushing
drop! as the fur falls from me and the man crashes, a crater,
from the heavens which he so adored and which I also decorate
as the forest of my regard. But now I have a larger following.

2
What spanking opossums of sneaks are caressing the routes!
and of the pulse-racked tremors attached to my viciousness
I can only enumerate the somber instances of wetness.

Is it a triumph? and are the lightnings of movedness
and abysmal elevation cantankerous filaments
of a larger faint-heartedness like loving summer? You,
accepting always the poisonous sting of the spine,
its golden efflorescence of nature which is distrustful,
how is one borne to this caprice of a lashing betrayal
whose jewel-like occasion has the clarity of blossoming trees?
is it not the deepest glitterings of love when the head
is turned off, glancing over a stranger's moonlike hatred
and finding an animal kingdom of jealousy in parachutes
descending upon the highway which you are not speeding down?
It is this silence which returns you to the open fields

of blandest red honey where the snake waits, his warm tongue.
Dice! into the lump and crush of archness and token angels
you burn your secret preferments and ancient streaming,

as a gasp of laughter at desire, and disorder, and dying.

3
And must I express the science of legendary elegies
consummate on the Clarissas of puma and gnu and wildebeest?
Blue negroes on the verge of a true foreignness
escape nevertheless the chromaticism of occidental death
by traffic, oh children bereaved of their doped carts
and priests with lips like mutton in their bedrooms at dawn!
and falling into a sea of asphalt abuse which is precisely life
in these provinces printed everywhere with the flag "Nobody,"
and these are the true tillers of the spirit
whose strangeness crushes in the only possible embrace,
is like splintering and pulling and draining the tooth
of the world, the violent alabaster yielding to the sky,
the kiss and the longing to be modern and sheltered and different
and insane and decorative as a Mayan idol too well understood
to be beautiful. Can roses be charming? As the sluice
pours forth its granular flayings a new cloud rises
and interplanetary driftings become simply initiatory gifts
like the circumcision of a black horse. I yield up
my lover to the reveries, completely, until he is taken away
by the demons who then deliver me their bolts from afar
like drunken Magi. It is the appeasement, frieze-style,
of undulant spiritual contamination, to which sainthood
I sacrifice my brilliant dryness, it had been my devoir
and my elegant distinction, a luminous enlacement
of the people through the bars of the zoo, the never fading.
My spirit is clouded, as it was in Tierra del Fuego,
and if the monsters who twirl on their toes like fiery wagons
cannot dismiss the oceanographer of a capricious promptness
which is more ethical than dismal, my heart
will break through to casualness and appear in windows
on Main Streets, "more vulgar but they love more than he

hates, as the apples turn straightway into balloons
and burst." No airship casts its shadow down the Road
of the Golden Arm, over which is folded the Canal
and the Shroud. A mystery appears and doesn't mention
intelligence or death, and is as swiftly gone into the corn
and the ivy fields, all red and grey in the gathering noise.
The houses look old, viscous, and their robes bear
massive pretenses to anxiety, the animal's dream
of successiveness, the paralytic's apprehension of germs,
and then, fleeing! the dancer's nestling into kelp
and the condemned man's amusement at versatility,
the judge's ardent approximation of harrowing languor
in which the pelt of the whole city moves forward as a flame.
One would call upon Apollo as a famous father and tenor
but the prodigious paleness of the insulted disfigures
all ingenuity and the sounds perfidious mountains move
away from with tomblike excitement, the eternal travelers,
so you are silent, aren't you? Well, I shall be older
and uglier than you, and my least motion shall wither
the vertiginous breath which is earth meeting sky meeting sea,
as in the legend of a sovereign who did and who was.
Immense flapping. I hold all of night in my one eye. You.

4
Is your throat dry with the deviousness of following?
I lead you to a stream which will lick you like a wasp,
and there the maidens will uncoil the hemp hunters and wires
so that your body may recline upon boards of starry nudging,
sisters of bar-girls in the haunches of the Himalayas.
Oh aspirations prancing like an elephant in a skirmish!
Or are you altitudes? . . .

5
                              or are you myself,
indifferent as a drunkard sponging off a car window?
Are you effeminate, like an eyelid, or are you feminine,
like a painting by Picasso? You fled when you followed,
and now the bamboo veils of intemperance are flapping down
with tigerish yaps over the paling corduroy doorway

which was once a capacious volute filled with airplanes,
and that was not a distance, that simple roaring and vagueness.
You are lean, achieved, ravished, acute, light, tan,
waving, stolen, lissome in whispering, salivary in intent,
similar to the sole support of a love affair, so artful,
and loyal only to faults. I found myself equal to every . . .

"Oh the droppings from the trees! the little clam shells,
their bosoms thrust into the clouds and kiss-stained!
I met Joe, his hair pale as the eyes of fields of maize
in August, at the gallery, he said you're the first Creon
of 1953, congrats. Your costume, he said, was hand
over fist. If you worked harder you could remake
old Barrymore movies, you're that statuesque, he said.
For when the window, the ice in it, ran, the fish leaped forth
and returned where they wished to return to and from,
as in a rainbow the end keeps leaping towards the middle
which is the shape of all flowers, and of all flowers
the most exotic." Yes! yes! it was cerulean, oh my darling!
"And the simple yet exquisite pertinence of that race
above the airfield, those tubby little planes flopping
competitively into the wind sleeve, was keen as a violin,
as colorless and as intent. It seemed there was no one there
but children, and at each flaming accident a crumbling giggle
tumbleweeded over the flats and into the hangars and echoed.
What must the fliers have thought? a performance
like a plate of ham and eggs eaten with a fur collar on.
I kept jingling the coins in my pocket and patting
the dollar bills that rustled like so many horses' hooves
against my anxious thigh. He was up there,
the one who ruined my sister while she was still a look
of spiritual withdrawal in my maiden aunt's memories
of bathing at Onset. I always win at Japanese bowling.
I won a piano with a flowered shawl draped over it
and a photograph of Anna Sten beside a trembling yellow vase."

Screaming and tearing at her breasts she bent over,
terribly pale and yet trifling with her feelings before him,

the heavy bronze crucifix he had stepped on, quite
accidentally, mistaking it for a moth, tinea pellionella,
which, in its labors against death, another more
vibrantly mournful kind, renders mankind subtly naked;
more than her eyes could stand, she went bloated into the azure
like a shot. Greying even more steadily now he remembered
the afternoon games of marbles beside the firehouse
and how the scum settled on his shoulders as he swam
and the many tasks done and forgotten and famous which,
as a pilot, he had disdained, trusting to luck always.
"Arabella" was the word he had muttered that moment
when lightning had smelled sweet over the zoo of the waves
while he played on and on and on and the women grew hysterical.
Of heldness and of caresses you have become the entrepreneur.
The sea looked like so many amethyst prophets and I,
hadn't the cannery sent forth perfume? would never go back.
And then staggering forward into the astounding capaciousness
of his own rumor he became violent as an auction,
rubbed the hairs on his chest with bottles of snarling
and deared the frying pan that curtained the windows
with his tears. I remember I felt at that moment the elephant
kissing. When paralysis becomes jaundice and jaundice
is blushing, a linen map of ecstasy hangs next the range
where the peas are burning and memories of Swan Lake
aspire like Victoria Falls to a jacket of dust.

You are too young to remember the lack of snow in 1953 showing:
"1 Except that you react like electricity to a chunk of cloth,
it will disappear like an ape at night. 2 Before eating
there was a closing of retina against retina, and ice,
telephone wires! was knotted, spelling out farce
which is germane to lust. 3 Then the historic duel in the surf
when black garments were wasted and swept over battlements
into the moat. 4 The book contained a rosary pressed
in the shape of a tongue. 5 The hill had begun to roll
luminously. A deck appeared among the fir trees. Larry's
uncle sent a missionary to India when he was in grade school
who cried 'Go straight' to the white men there. Forgiveness

of heat. 6 Green lips pressed his body like a pearl shell.
7 It all took place in darkness, and meant more earlier
when they were in different places and didn't know each other.
As is often misprinted.'' And such whiteness not there!
All right, all right, all right, you glass of coke, empty
your exceptionally neonish newspaper from such left hands
with headlines to be grey as cut WITHER ACCEPTED AS SELLING.
(The western mountain ranges were sneaking along "Who
taps wires and why?" like a pack of dogies and is there much
tapping under the desert moon? Does it look magical
or realistic, that landing? And the riverboat put in there,
keeps putting in, with all the slaves' golden teeth and arms,
self-conscious without their weapons. Joe LeSueur,
the handsome Captain who smuggles Danish perfumes, tied up
at the arroyo and with thunderous hooves swam across a causeway
to make the Honest Dollar. In Pasadena they are calling
"Higho, Silver!" but in the High Sierras they just shoot
movie after movie. Who is "they"? The Westerners, of course,
the tans. Didn't you ever want to be a cowboy, buster?) Big-
town papers, you see, and this great-coated tour of the teens
in (oh bless me!) imagination. That's what the snow said,
"and doesn't your penis look funny today?" I jacked "off."

6
"Nous avons eu lundi soir, le grand plaisir de rencontrer
à l'Hôtel Oloffson où elle est descendue, la charmante
Mlle. Anne R. Lang, actrice du Théâtre Dramatique de Cambridge.
Miss Lang est arrivée à Port-au-Prince le mardi 24 février
à bord d'un avion de la 'Resort Air Line.'
Cette belle artiste a visité les sites de la Capitale
et est enchantée de tout ce qu'elle a vu. Elle est fort
éprise de notre pays." And it's very exciting to be an old friend
of Verlaine and he has his problems, divine dust bag
of pressure chambers which is merely an episode clarifying
what the work really is in relationship with birds and insects
you are sitting on as you drink and think about dancing,
poor dedicated blonde that you are, ma fille, ma soeur,
my fellow airlines provocateur and sandal dropper on the hots.

Do you know which back alley we would park and snot the wimple
in? It is embarrassing to be too rich with black looks,
he would be waiting for you to come in from roaming, slipper
in left hand raised, the famous left hand of the epigraph.
"Ah, oui." Tumbling vipers where your stain, Lar, hot-tranced
into the hydrogen of a backache which is a whole harem
of swaying odors and caravanserai grit, alors! c'est mung,
the middling passionate rapids down where a tender word
rushes to snarl and laugh deliriously into the back of the head
where the hair barnacles its uneasy lay against the nape
so ecstatic, like churchbells against the flanks of horsetails,
sleight of hand, "Ô reine Überschreigung!" of an old lavatory.
It was that way many times, yet the winter seemed prompt.

7
"You come to me smelling of the shit of Pyrrhian maidens!
and I as a fast come-on for fascinating fleas-in-ice
become ravenously casual avec quel haut style de chambre!
and deny myself every pasture of cerise cumulus cries.
You yourself had taken out volumes of rare skies' pillars
and then bowed forth screaming 'Lindy Has Made It!' until
everyone showed their teeth to the neighbors of Uncle,
how embarrassing! the whiteness of the imitation of the glass
in which one elegant pig had straddled a pheasant and wept.
Well enough. To garner the snowing snow and then leave,
what an inspiration! as if suddenly, while dancing, someone,
a rather piratish elderly girl, had stuck her fan up her ass
and then become a Chinese legend before the bullrushes ope'd.
Yet I became aware of history as rods stippling the dip
of a fancied and intuitive scientific roadmap, clarté et
volupté et vif! swooping over the valley and under the lavender
where children prayed and had stillborn blue brothers of
entirely other races, the Tour Babel, as they say, said.
I want listeners to be distracted, as fur rises when most needed
and walks away to be another affair on another prairie,
yowee, it's heaven in Heaven! with the leaves falling
like angels who've been discharged for sodomy
and it all almost over, that is too true to last, that is,

'rawther old testament, dontcha know.' When they bite,
you've never seen anything more beautiful, the sheer fantail
of it and them delicately clinging to the crimson box
like so many squid, for sweetness. Do you have the haveness
of a collapse, of a rummaging albatross that sings? No!
don't even consider asking me to the swimming team's tea-
and-alabaster breakfast. I just don't want to be asked."

The mountains had trembled, quivering as if about to withdraw,
and where the ships had lined up on the frontier waiting for
the first gunshot, a young girl lunched on aspergum. A cow
belched. The sun went. Later in the day Steven farted.
He dropped his torpedo into the bathtub. Flowers. Relativity.
He stayed under water 65 seconds the first time and 84 the second.
Sheer Olympia, the last of the cat-lovers, oh Jimmy!
the prettiest cat in New York. A waiter stole the dollar bill
while the people sang in the Cicada Circle built in 1982
at a cost of three rose petals. She told him she'd miss him
when she went to live in the marshgrass, did Berdie,
and he thought, "You'll miss me like that emerald I have at home
I forgot to give you when I lost my pink Birthday Book
when it was smuggled out of Europe in a box of chocolate-cherries."
Thirty-five cancerous growths were removed from as many breasts
in one great iron-grill-work purple apartment house yesterday,
and this tribute to the toughness of the Air Corps is like rain.

Had not all beautiful things become real on Wednesday?
and had not your own bumbleshoot caressed a clergyman and autos?
To be sure, the furniture was wrinkled, but a cat doesn't wink,
and her motto exists on the Liberian Ambassador's stationery,
"Amor vincit et Cicero vidit" in sachets of morning-glories.

8
Candidly. The past, the sensations of the past. Now!
in cuneiform, of umbrella satrap square-carts with hotdogs
and onions of red syrup blended, of sand bejewelling the prepuce
in tank suits, of Majestic Camera Stores and Schuster's,

of Kenneth in an abandoned storeway on Sunday cutting ever more
insinuating lobotomies of a yet-to-be-more-yielding world
of ears, of a soprano rallying at night in a cadenza, Bill, of
"Fornications, la! garumph! tereu! lala la! vertigo! Weevy! Hah!",
of a limp hand larger than the knee which seems to say "Addio"
and is capable of resigning from the disaster it summoned ashore.
Acres of glass don't make the sign clearer of the landscape
less blue than prehistorically, yet less distant, eager, dead!
and generations of thorns are reconstructed as a mammoth
unstitched from the mighty thigh of the glacier, the Roaring Id.
You remained for me a green Buick of sighs, o Gladstone!
and your wife Trina, how like a yellow pillow on a sill
in the many-windowed dusk where the air is compartmented!
her red lips of Hollywood, soft as a Titian and as tender,
her grey face which refrains from thrusting aside the mane
of your languorous black smells, the hand crushed by her chin,
and that slumberland of dark cutaneous lines which reels
under the burden of her many-darkly-hued corpulence of linen
and satin bushes, is like a lone rose with the sky behind it.
A yellow rose. Valentine's Day. "Imagine that substance
extended for two hours of theatre and you see the inevitable,
the disappearance of vigor in a heart not sufficiently basted
or burnt, the mere apparition of feeling in an empty bedroom.
Zounds!! you want money? Take my watch which is always fast."

Accuracy has never envisaged itself as occurring; rather a
negligence, royal in retreating upwards of the characteristics
of multitudes. "You call me Mamie, but I'm monickered Sanskrit
in the San Remo, and have a divorce inside my lamé left breast,"
so into the headlands where the peaceful aborigines eat the meat
that's always white, no muscles, no liver, no brains, no, no,
tongue, that's it. Weary. Well, forgetting you not is forgetting,
even if I think of you tall the day, and forgetting you is
forgiving you not, for I am weeping from a tall wet dream, oh.
Cantankerous month! have you ever moved more slowly into surf?
Oh Bismarck! Fortitude! exceptional delights of intelligence!
yappings at cloister doors! dimpled marshmallows! oh March!

9

Now in November, by Josephine Johnson. The Heroes,
by John Ashbery. Topper's Roumanian Broilings. The Swimmer.
Your feet are more beautiful than your father's, I think,
does that upset you? admire, I admire youth above age, yes,
in the infancy of the race when we were very upset we wrote,
"O toe!" and it took months to "get" those feet. Render. Rent.
Now more features of our days have become popular, the nose
broken, the head bald, the body beautiful. Marilyn Monroe.
Can one's lips be "more" or "less" sensual? "Ma,
il primo bacio debbo darlo ancora," so which of you banditti
knows? oh braggarts! toothpastes! you motherfuckers! At
lunch in the park the pigeons are like tulips on the trees.

O panic of drying mushrooms! how many gorillas are there
in cages? They are bashing the seals over the head with coke.
As I walked into the Dairy B & H Lunch I couldn't remember
your other eye, I puked. Sunday came, the violet waves crusted.
The sand bristled and with its stinging flashes we dove
screaming into the rocks where pythons nestled and brooded.
Is the nose, for instance, part of the forehead, a strawberry
part of the forest? Bill was married secretly by a Negro justice
over the Savoy on Massachusetts Avenue where I met for beer
my lover on secret Sundays, for we were all very young
and needed a headquarters which became a jazz tree-hut.
Don't forget, you're most alone, Caramba! Optimo!
when you're alone, when yellow and blue lumber's piled on
a sledge and you gee and haw the oxen as the spring circles
warily and the pheasants shit. Jack-in-the-Pulpit. Bailey
Whitney. My father said, "Do what you want but don't get hurt,
I'm warning you. Leave the men alone, they'll only tease you.
When your aunt comes I want you to get down off that horse
and speak like a gentleman, or I'll take it away from you.
Don't grit your teeth at me." A chicken walked by with tail
reared, looking very personal, pecking and dribbling, wattles.
You suddenly got an idea of what black and white poetry
was like, you grinning Simian fart, poseur among idiots
and dilettantes and pederasts. When the chips are in,

yours will spell out in a wealth of dominoes, YOU, and you'll
be stuck with it, hell to anybody else, drowning in lead,
like your brain, of which the French poets wrote, "O fat-assed
configurations and volutions of ribbed sand which the sea
never reaches!" Memories of home, which is an island, of course,
and historical, of course, and full of ass, of course. Yes,
may you trip on a blue fire-escape and go up when it's raining!
what dismal monster cannot be electrocuted? what fool
not rumpled? what miserable wretch not forced upon the happiness
which kills? I witnessed at last the calmness of ordure.

Less comfortable but more decorative. My head covered
by a green cloth. Taxicabs whistling by. Fulgently leaning
from behind, slightly bent. And then the paralyzing rush
of emotion, its fists caught in Venetian blinds, silent,
burgeoning, like a smudge-pot in a tornado. Utica Avenue.
"Arrivaderlà!" Chief Dispursing Officer, Division of
Disbursement. "I'm glad there's something beautiful in his life."
Shall I ever be able to avail myself of the service called
"Same Day Cleaning," and in what face have I fought the Host?

10
The silence that lasted for a quarter of a century. All
the babies were born blue. They called him "Al" and "Horseballs"
in kindergarten, he had an autocratic straw face like a dark
in a de Kooning where the torrent has subsided at the very center
of classicism, it can be many whirlpools in a gun battle
or each individual pang in the "last mile" of electrodes, so
totally unlike xmas tree ornaments that you wonder, uhmmm?
what the bourgeoisie is thinking off. Trench coat. Broken strap.
Pseudo-aggressive as the wife of a psychiatrist. Beating off.
Banging off. It is delicately thorough in laying its leaden sneer
down in Brettschneider's Funeral Home. You'll say I'm supper,
naturally, but one is distinguished by the newspapers of the lips.

"He vaporously nags down the quoits. I might have to suffer
for another year. I might severally dismiss my trysts, la!
as the fire-eaters collide. See, lumbering dimly: the quest

for Japanese deer, lazy, mean, truncated. See not the ray.
Jealousy bans raffles, lumia advances, ditto March's amber,
pending quietly Negro lariat tumbling derailed 'de' whores.
Jumping ripples pour forth Rienzi. A present: community, Alp,
a jiffy immune piping in a boat of vice about dumbness.
My villain accommodates a Chinese scent to jar the bone-on,
maybe jetting beasts parse what we hesitantly choose,
nipping oval appetites changing and quieting in a Paris
of voluptuary chases, lays, choices, what we know and savor.
Perk quietly, don't, pension me and ply me with love that's droll,
noose light harms and nutty bathers, use, nip, alarm and pet,
eat, sup, end, Antinous, lake of comprehension, unless passion
down aimlessly sonorous plusses, denies our doubtful paroles,"

says that the show miserably disturbs, the endurance of water,
and when the pressure asphyxiates and inflames, Grace destroys
the whirling faces in their dissonant gaiety where it's anxious,
lifted nasally to the heavens which is a carrousel grinning
and spasmodically obliterated with loaves of greasy white paint
and this becomes like love to her, is what I desire
and what you, to be able to throw something away without yawning
"Oh Leaves of Grass! o Sylvette! oh Basket Weavers' Conference!"
and thus make good our promise to destroy something but not us.
A green fire-escape, an orange fire-escape, a black, a grey spider.
"Dolores, O hobble and kobble Dolores. O perfect obstruction
on track." See? "Je suis reine de Sparte et celle-là de Troie,
sachant quels gras couchants ont les plus blancs aveux?"
O pain! driftwood and limewood, they kissed, were missing a leg.
And yet the simple endurance of their attraction carried a camel
into the lake formerly placarded "Abyss of Sizzling Tears."

Butter. Lotions. Cries. A glass of ice. Aldebaran and Mizar,
a guitar of toothpaste tubes and fingernails, trembling spear.
Balustrade, tensile, enclosing the surging waters of my heart
in a laughing collapse where the natives tint urine their hair:
trolley cars find cat-eyes in New Guinea where Mozart died,
on the beach fraught with emotion and rotting elephants,
that elephant of a smile which lingers when I lean over and throw.

11
My hands are Massimo Plaster, called "White Pin in the Arm of the Sea"
and I'm blazoned and scorch like a fleet of windbells down the Pulaski Skyway,
tabletops of Vienna carrying their bundles of cellophane to the laundry,
ear to the tongue, glistening semester of ardency, young-old daringnesses
at the foot of the most substantial art product of our times,
the world, the jongleurs, fields of dizzyness and dysentery
before reaching Mexico, the palace of stammering sinking success
before billows of fangs, red faces, orange eyebrows, green, yes! ears,
O paradise! my airplanes known as "Banana Line Incorporealidad,"
saviors of connections and spit, dial HYacinth 9-9945, "Isn't that
a conundrum?" asked him Sydney Burger, humming "Mein' Yiddisher Mama,"
I emulate the black which is a cry but is not voluptuary like a warning,
which has lines, cuts, drips, aspirates, trembles with horror,
O black looks at the base of the spine! kisses on the medulla oblongata
of an inky clarity! always the earlobes in the swiftest bird's-death
of night, the snarl of expiation which is the skirt of Hercules,
and the remorse in the desert shouts "Flea! Bonanza! Cheek! Teat!
Elbow of roaches! You wear my white rooster like a guerdon in vales
of Pompeiian desires, before utter languorousness puts down its chisel,"
and the desert is here. "You've reached the enormous summit of passion
which is immobility forging an entrail from the pure obstruction of the air."

ON RACHMANINOFF'S BIRTHDAY

Quick! a last poem before I go
off my rocker. Oh Rachmaninoff!
Onset, Massachusetts. Is it the fig-newton
playing the horn? Thundering windows
of hell, will your tubes ever break
into powder? Oh my palace of oranges,

junk shop, staples, umber, basalt;
I'm a child again when I was really
miserable, a grope pizzicato. My pocket
of rhinestone, yoyo, carpenter's pencil,
amethyst, hypo, campaign button,
is the room full of smoke? Shit
on the soup, let it burn. So it's back.
You'll never be mentally sober.

ROMANZE, OR THE MUSIC STUDENTS

1
The rain, its tiny pressure
on your scalp, like ants
passing the door of a tobacconist.
"Hello!" they cry, their noses
glistening. They are humming
a scherzo by Tcherepnin.
They are carrying violin cases.
With their feelers knitting
over their heads the blue air,
they appear at the door of
the Conservatory and cry "Ah!"
at the honey of its outpourings.
They stand in the street and hear
the curds drifting on the top
of the milk of Conservatory doors.

2
They had thought themselves
in Hawaii when suddenly the pines,
trembling with nightfulness,

shook them out of their sibilance.
The surf was full of outriggers
racing like slits in the eye of
the sun, yet the surf was full
of great black logs plunging, and
then the surf was full of needles.
The surf was bland and white,
as pine trees are white when,
in Paradise, no wind is blowing.

3
In Ann Arbor on Sunday afternoon
at four-thirty they went to an organ
recital: Messiaen, Hindemith, Czerny.
And in their ears a great voice said
"To have great music we must commission
it. To commission great music
we must have great commissioners."
There was a blast! and summer was over.

4
Rienzi! A rabbit is sitting in the hedge!
it is a brown stone! it is the month
of October! it is an orange bassoon!
They've been standing on this mountain
for forty-eight hours without flinching.
Well, they are soldiers, I guess,
and it is all marching magnificently by.

THE HUNTER

He set out and kept hunting
and hunting. Where, he thought
and thought, is the real chamois?
and can I kill it where it is?
He had brought with him only a dish
of pears. The autumn wind soared
above the trails where the drops
of the chamois led him further.
The leaves dropped around him
like pie-plates. The stars fell
one by one into his eyes and burnt.

There is a geography which holds
its hands just so far from the breast
and pushes you away, crying so.
He went on to strange hills where
the stones were still warm from feet,
and then on and on. There were clouds
at his knees, his eyelashes
had grown thick from the colds,
as the fur of the bear does
in winter. Perhaps, he thought, I am
asleep, but he did not freeze to death.

There were little green needles
everywhere. And then manna fell.
He knew, above all, that he was now
approved, and his strength increased.
He saw the world below him, brilliant
as a floor, and steaming with gold,
with distance. There were occasionally
rifts in the cloud where the face
of a woman appeared, frowning. He
had gone higher. He wore ermine.

He thought, why did I come? and then,
I have come to rule! The chamois came.

The chamois found him and they came
in droves to humiliate him. Alone,
in the clouds, he was humiliated.

THE SPIRIT INK

Prince of calm, treasure of fascinating cuts on my arm,
an x ill-aims its roguish atonal bliss of "ment"
and hatted is the viper whose illness I hated having to puke,
April in the lavatory trouble, inside the air he deceives.

Rover! cheat the scholars, Dubonnet Sir Pint,
oust his slick offer to bow, eat, touch your eyes upon.
Park the lily and quietly knit the loose air of a purse,
tough ass, dissembler and fool, O syrup of mammoths!

TO JANE; AND IN IMITATION OF COLERIDGE

All fears, all doubts and even dreams
that parody my slender frame
are driven from me, and their screams,
     by the mere thought of fame.

When I stare and brood, and I do often,
I walk again through mountain air
where terrible winds did suddenly soften
    at invisible music there,

or far at sea I once more capture
men and cities and whales in rain,
yet can't make serious with my rapture
    slyly thoughtful, smiling Jane,

who does not feel the sky's a clock
nor that the sea will swallow me—
though she would feel alone, in shock,
    if I did drown, could no more see

her smiling face that sorrows leave
whenever she despatches care,
and she can not unless I grieve
    that she's preoccupied there.

She thinks of me as melancholy,
I think of her as bright and sad,
often my pretentious folly
    makes me self-ashamed and bad

but never to her, never to Jane
"with downcast Eyes and modest Grace";
I could from fame's blue heights refrain
    but never from her blue-lit face.

Her slender hands accomplish more
in moving from sheet to telephone
than all the burning shields knights bore,
    dull blows or slashings to the bone.

I never tell her this because
embarrassment is far more fatal
than shrouding verse in Romantic gauze
    or voyagings foolish and prenatal.

And I am all at sea, at war,
if I ever had a chance I left it
there on the iron deck, my star:
      I stride upon, but cannot heft it.

But I should be master of my ship
not just a member of the crew!
though she may think that I will slip
      into insanity and the blue,

I will not, for I more and more
am master of myself each day,
and sometimes from a savage shore
      plunge into surf and swim away,

and sometimes on my sulking face
a green and sunny look I see
and I fight towards it o'er what space
      the deck's obstruction thrusts at me.

And if her face, my sky, hold fast,
do not abandon nor disdain!
the vessel shall be mine at last,
      as if my life were after Jane.

I do not know how in the South
I managed to content myself
with salt and Mozart in my mouth
      on the Pacific like a shelf

crowded and lonely and overreachable,
low the clouds and light the moon,
low as heaven and as teachable
      as Christianity in its June,

or how in New England where I grew
and tried both to fight and to escape,
I thrived without her intimate view
      always before me, my seascape;

for as the war, art, dissipation,
led me on and made me sane,
I find a world of sweet sensation
    leading me now, and it is Jane.

She is the Lady of my Lake,
the Lily of my sordid life,
hatred within me, for her sake,
    noiselessly empties like a fife

played often but above her hearing
not her tranquility to alarm,
rather t' oppose, by scale endearing,
    the extremity of her charm.

Never her bosom, that soft booty,
's seen in the sea of a sheltered bay,
but that the daughters of Albion's beauty
    in pure consciousness fades away;

she half incloses worlds in her eyes,
she moves as the wind is said to blow,
she watches motions of the skies
    as if she were everywhere to go.

" 'Twas partly Love, and partly Fear,
And partly 'twas a bashful Art"—
the poet cannot hope to near
    the mysterious clarity of her heart;

she is not dangerous or rare,
adventure precedes her like a train,
her beauty is general, as sun and air
    are secretly near, like Jane.

TO A POET

I am sober and industrious
and would be plain and plainer
for a little while
                    until my rococo
self is more assured of its
distinction.
            So you do not like
my new verses, written in the
pages of Russian novels while I do
not brood over an orderly
childhood?
            You are angry
because I see the white-haired
genius of the painter more beautiful
than the stammering vivacity

                          of
your temperament. And yes,
it becomes more and more a matter
of black and white between us

and when the doctor comes to
me he says "No things but in ideas"
or it is overheard
                    in the public
square, now that I am off my couch.

AUS EINEM APRIL

We dust the walls.
And of course we are weeping larks
falling all over the heavens with our shoulders clasped
in someone's armpits, so tightly! and our throats are full.
Haven't you ever fallen down at Christmas
and didn't it move everyone who saw you?
isn't that what the tree means? the pure pleasure
of making weep those whom you cannot move by your flights!
It's enough to drive one to suicide.
And the rooftops are falling apart like the applause

of rough, long-nailed, intimate, roughened-by-kisses, hands.
Fingers more breathless than a tongue laid upon the lips
in the hour of sunlight, early morning, before the mist rolls
in from the sea; and out there everything is turbulent and green.

SPLEEN

I know so much
about things, I accept
so much, it's like
vomiting. And I am
nourished by the
shabbiness of my
knowing so much
about others and what
they do, and accepting

so much that I hate
as if I didn't know
what it is, to me.
And what it is to
them I know, and hate.

KITVILLE

Sands, sunset, toilets,
O the charities!
the little asylums
of the verities

Once I was humbled
amidst the flowers
and her crushed books
were like bloomers!

She was reading clear
by the coffee lake
and its bitter springs
were a bubbling brook,

and garish her lips
as they parted! a piano
of grassy incidents
twined with the liana

of her wet arms!
behind the bath house
sweet as a wash basin,
her smilings, her pathos.

ON RACHMANINOFF'S BIRTHDAY

Blue windows, blue rooftops
and the blue light of the rain,
these contiguous phrases of Rachmaninoff
pouring into my enormous ears
and the tears falling into my blindness

for without him I do not play,
especially in the afternoon
on the day of his birthday. Good
fortune, you would have been
my teacher and I your only pupil

and I would always play again.
Secrets of Liszt and Scriabin
whispered to me over the keyboard
on unsunny afternoons! and growing
still in my stormy heart.

Only my eyes would be blue as I played
and you rapped my knuckles,
dearest father of all the Russias,
placing my fingers
tenderly upon your cold, tired eyes.

POEM IN JANUARY

March, the fierce! like a wind of garters
its calm kept secret, as if eaten!
and sipped at the source tainted, taut.

Vagrants, crushed by such effulgence,
wrap their mild twigs and bruises in straws
and touch themselves tightly, like buttered bees,

for the sun is cold, there, as an eyeglass
playing with its freshly running sinuses,
swampy, and of a molasses sweetness on the cheek.

Turn, oh turn! your pure divining rod
for the sake of infantile suns and their railing
and storming at the deplorably pale cheeks

and the hemlocks not yet hung up.
Do we live in old, sane, sensible cries?
The guards stand up and down like a waltz

and its strains are stolen by fauns
with their wounded feet nevertheless dashing
away through the woods, for the iris! for autumn!

Oh pure blue of a footstep, have you stolen
March? and, with your cupiditous baton
struck agog? do you feel that you have, blue?

Ah, March! you have not decided whom you train.
Or what traitors are waiting for you to be born,
oh March! or what it will mean in terms of diet.

Take my clear big eyes into your heart, and then
pump my clear big eyes through your bloodstream, and!
stick my clear big eyes on your feet, it is cold,

I am all over snowshoes and turning round
and round. There's a trail of blood through
the wood and a few shreds of faun-colored hair.

I am troubled as I salute the crocus.
There shall be no more reclining on the powdered roads,
your veins are using up the redness of the world.

MY HEAT

If, jetting, I committed the noble fault
turning in air fell off the balcony
to refountain myself I'd force the port!
violate the piers and their bushy moorings
      you bores! you asses!

geology?   that's hefting the crop
rats like me so profoundly trust;
if I jet into the azure breeze
to multiply the roses there
      I'm roseate myself, aren't I?

and if I jet a grinning conspiracy
to melt everyone into syrup
and feel sure I am that second volcano
and decide that I'm Vesuvius
      you'll say "Itself?"

if I'm jetting rather putridly one
day, you'll say "give me your volcanic
papers, Frank, make peace" but
I'll be dangerous as bread that day,
      I discovered penicillin

or if I'm lying in the harbor quietly
jetting on my back and a refrigerator ship
sails in "for the love of God, Frank
make me your little igloo, I'm on fire!"
      you'd hate my compassion

you'd quit because you can't appreciate
how rich the volcanic appetite, essentially, is—
in regulating my soul's beneficence
I've kayoed your popular cant
      I'd rather jet!

I'm laughing like an old bedspring;
a rather glamorous priest behind the curtains
is groping for benignity, ha! he can't take
that away from me—*Miserere, Domine*
      what a grumbler!

for if you have duennas of children
or of ugliness, I just give up, I throw
myself back into the bay—the sun spits
and I spit back, or maybe we both pour:
      "That's no furnace, that's my heart!"

ODE

    An idea of justice may be precious,
    one vital gregarious amusement . . .

What are you amused by? a crisis
like a cow being put on the payroll
with the concomitant investigations and divinings?
Have you swept the dung from the tracks?
    Am I a door?
If millions criticize you for drinking too much,
the cow is going to look like Venus and you'll make a pass
yes, you and your friend from High School,
the basketball player whose black eyes exceed yours
as he picks up the ball with one hand.
    But doesn't he doubt, too?

    To be equal? it's the worst!
    Are we just muddy instants?

No, you must treat me like a fox; or, being a child,
kill the oriole though it reminds you of me.
Thus you become the author of all being. Women
    unite against you.

It's as if I were carrying a horse on my shoulders
and I couldn't see his face. His iron legs
hang down to the earth on either side of me
like the arch of triumph in Washington Square.
I would like to beat someone with him
but I can't get him off my shoulders, he's like evening.

Evening! your breeze is an obstacle,
    it changes me, I am being arrested,
        and if I mock you into a face
and, disgusted, throw down the horse—ah! there's his face!
and I am, sobbing, walking on my heart.

        I want to take your hands off my hips
        and put them on a statue's hips;

then I can thoughtfully regard the justice of your feelings
for me, and, changing, regard my own love for you
as beautiful. I'd never cheat you and say "It's inevitable!"
        It's just barely natural.
        But we do course together
like two battleships maneuvering away from the fleet.
I am moved by the multitudes of your intelligence
and sometimes, returning, I become the sea—
in love with your speed, your heaviness and breath.

Am I to become profligate as if I were a blonde? Or religious as if I were French?

Each time my heart is broken it makes me feel more adventurous (and how the same names keep recurring on that interminable list!), but one of these days there'll be nothing left with which to venture forth.

Why should I share you? Why don't you get rid of someone else for a change?

I am the least difficult of men. All I want is boundless love.

Even trees understand me! Good heavens, I lie under them, too, don't I? I'm just like a pile of leaves.

However, I have never clogged myself with the praises of pastoral life, nor with nostalgia for an innocent past of perverted acts in pastures. No. One need never leave the confines of New York to get all the greenery one wishes—I can't even enjoy a blade of grass unless I know there's a subway handy, or a record store or some other sign that people do not totally *regret* life. It is more important to affirm the least sincere; the clouds get enough attention as it is and even they continue to pass. Do they know what they're missing? Uh huh.

My eyes are vague blue, like the sky, and change all the time; they are indiscriminate but fleeting, entirely specific and disloyal, so that no one trusts me. I am always looking away. Or again at something after it has given me up. It makes me restless and that makes me unhappy, but I cannot keep them still. If only I had grey, green, black, brown, yellow eyes; I would stay at home and do something. It's not that I'm curious. On the contrary, I am bored but it's my duty to be attentive, I am needed by things as the sky must be above the earth. And lately, so great has *their* anxiety become, I can spare myself little sleep.

Now there is only one man I love to kiss when he is unshaven. Heterosexuality! you are inexorably approaching. (How discourage her?)

St. Serapion, I wrap myself in the robes of your whiteness which is like midnight in Dostoevsky. How am I to become a legend, my dear? I've tried love, but that hides you in the bosom of another and I am always springing forth from it like the lotus—the ecstasy of always bursting forth! (but one must not be distracted by it!) or like a hyacinth, "to keep the filth of life away," yes, there, even in the heart, where the filth is pumped in and slanders and pollutes and determines. I will my will, though I may become famous for a mysterious vacancy in that department, that greenhouse.

Destroy yourself, if you don't know!

It is easy to be beautiful; it is difficult to appear so. I admire you, beloved, for the trap you've set. It's like a final chapter no one reads because the plot is over.

"Fanny Brown is run away—scampered off with a Cornet of Horse; I do love that little Minx, & hope She may be happy, tho' She has vexed me by this Exploit a little too. —Poor silly Cecchina! or F:B: as we used to call her. —I wish She had a good Whipping and 10,000 pounds." —Mrs. Thrale.

I've got to get out of here. I choose a piece of shawl and my dirtiest suntans. I'll be back, I'll re-emerge, defeated, from the valley; you don't want me to go where you go, so I go where you don't want me to. It's only afternoon, there's a lot ahead. There won't be any mail downstairs. Turning, I spit in the lock and the knob turns.

MAYAKOVSKY

1
My heart's aflutter!
I am standing in the bath tub
crying. Mother, mother
who am I? If he

will just come back once
and kiss me on the face
his coarse hair brush
my temple, it's throbbing!

then I can put on my clothes
I guess, and walk the streets.

2
I love you. I love you,
but I'm turning to my verses
and my heart is closing
like a fist.

Words! be
sick as I am sick, swoon,
roll back your eyes, a pool,

and I'll stare down
at my wounded beauty
which at best is only a talent
for poetry.

Cannot please, cannot charm or win
what a poet!
and the clear water is thick

with bloody blows on its head.
I embraced a cloud,
but when I soared
it rained.

3
That's funny! there's blood on my chest
oh yes, I've been carrying bricks
what a funny place to rupture!
and now it is raining on the ailanthus
as I step out onto the window ledge

the tracks below me are smoky and
glistening with a passion for running
I leap into the leaves, green like the sea

4
Now I am quietly waiting for
the catastrophe of my personality
to seem beautiful again,
and interesting, and modern.

The country is grey and
brown and white in trees,
snows and skies of laughter
always diminishing, less funny
not just darker, not just grey.

It may be the coldest day of
the year, what does he think of
that? I mean, what do I? And if I do,
perhaps I am myself again.

(JULY IS OVER AND THERE'S VERY LITTLE TRACE)

July is over and there's very little trace
of it, though the Bastille fell on its face—

and August's gotten orange, it will drop on
the edge of the world like a worm-eaten sun.

The trees are taking off their leaves. So
the purity of the streets is coming, low,

in white waves. In the summer I got good and sunburnt,
winter, so I wouldn't miss the wet brunt

of your storms. Then it was sand from the surf
in my bathing trunks; now snow fills up my scarf.

MUSIC

      If I rest for a moment near The Equestrian
pausing for a liver sausage sandwich in the Mayflower Shoppe,
that angel seems to be leading the horse into Bergdorf's
and I am naked as a table cloth, my nerves humming.
Close to the fear of war and the stars which have disappeared.
I have in my hands only 35¢, it's so meaningless to eat!
and gusts of water spray over the basins of leaves
like the hammers of a glass pianoforte. If I seem to you
to have lavender lips under the leaves of the world,
      I must tighten my belt.
It's like a locomotive on the march, the season
      of distress and clarity
and my door is open to the evenings of midwinter's
lightly falling snow over the newspapers.
Clasp me in your handkerchief like a tear, trumpet
of early afternoon! in the foggy autumn.
As they're putting up the Christmas trees on Park Avenue
I shall see my daydreams walking by with dogs in blankets,
put to some use before all those coloured lights come on!
      But no more fountains and no more rain,
        and the stores stay open terribly late.

FOR GRACE, AFTER A PARTY

You do not always know what I am feeling.
Last night in the warm spring air while I was
blazing my tirade against someone who doesn't
interest
          me, it was love for you that set me
afire,
          and isn't it odd? for in rooms full of
strangers my most tender feelings
                              writhe and
bear the fruit of screaming. Put out your hand,
isn't there
          an ashtray, suddenly, there? beside
the bed? And someone you love enters the room
and says wouldn't
                    you like the eggs a little
different today?
                    And when they arrive they are
just plain scrambled eggs and the warm weather
is holding.

POEM

I watched an armory combing its bronze bricks
and in the sky there were glistening rails of milk.
Where had the swan gone, the one with the lame back?

Now mounting the steps
I enter my new home full
of grey radiators and glass
ashtrays full of wool.

Against the winter I must get a samovar
embroidered with basil leaves and Ukranian mottos
to the distant sound of wings, painfully anti-wind,

       a little bit of the blue
       summer air will come back
       as the steam chuckles in
       the monster's steamy attack

and I'll be happy here and happy there, full
of tea and tears. I don't suppose I'll ever get
to Italy, but I have the terrible tundra at least.

       My new home will be full
       of wood, roots and the like,
       while I pace in a turtleneck
       sweater, repairing my bike.

I watched the palisades shivering in the snow
of my face, which had grown preternaturally pure.
Once I destroyed a man's idea of himself to have him.

       If I'd had a samovar then
       I'd have made him tea
       and as hyacinths grow from
       a pot he would love me

and my charming room of tea cosies full of dirt
which is why I must travel, to collect the leaves.
O my enormous piano, you are not like being outdoors

       though it is cold and you
       are made of fire and wood!

I lift your lid and mountains
return, that I am good.

The stars blink like a hairnet that was dropped
on a seat and now it is lying in the alley behind
the theater where my play is echoed by dying voices.

I am really a woodcarver
and my words are love
which willfully parades in
its room, refusing to move.

POEM

To James Schuyler

There I could never be a boy,
though I rode like a god when the horse reared.
At a cry from mother I fell to my knees!
there I fell, clumsy and sick and good,
though I bloomed on the back of a frightened black mare
who had leaped windily at the start of a leaf
and she never threw me.

I had a quick heart
and my thighs clutched her back.
I loved her fright, which was against me
into the air! and the diamond white of her forelock
which seemed to smart with thoughts as my heart smarted with life!
and she'd toss her head with the pain
and paw the air and champ the bit, as if I were Endymion
and she, moonlike, hated to love me.

All things are tragic
when a mother watches!
and she wishes upon herself
the random fears of a scarlet soul, as it breathes in and out
and nothing chokes, or breaks from triumph to triumph!

I knew her but I could not be a boy,
for in the billowing air I was fleet and green
riding blackly through the ethereal night
towards men's words which I gracefully understood,

and it was given to me
as the soul is given the hands
to hold the ribbons of life!
as miles streak by beneath the moon's sharp hooves
and I have mastered the speed and strength which is the armor of the world.

TO THE HARBORMASTER

I wanted to be sure to reach you;
though my ship was on the way it got caught
in some moorings. I am always tying up
and then deciding to depart. In storms and
at sunset, with the metallic coils of the tide
around my fathomless arms, I am unable
to understand the forms of my vanity
or I am hard alee with my Polish rudder
in my hand and the sun sinking. To
you I offer my hull and the tattered cordage
of my will. The terrible channels where
the wind drives me against the brown lips

of the reeds are not all behind me. Yet
I trust the sanity of my vessel; and
if it sinks, it may well be in answer
to the reasoning of the eternal voices,
the waves which have kept me from reaching you.

FOR JAMES DEAN

Welcome me, if you will,
as the ambassador of a hatred
who knows its cause
and does not envy you your whim
of ending him.

For a young actor I am begging
peace, gods. Alone
in the empty streets of New York
I am its dirty feet and head
and he is dead.

He has banged into your wall
of air, your hubris, racing
towards your heights and you
have cut him from your table
which is built, how unfairly
for us! not on trees, but on clouds.

I speak as one whose filth
is like his own, of pride
and speed and your terrible
example nearer than the sirens' speech,

a spirit eager for the punishment
which is your only recognition.

Peace! to be true to a city
of rats and to love the envy
of the dreary, smudged mouthers
of an arcane dejection
smoldering quietly in the perception
of hopelessness and scandal
at unnatural vigor. Their dreams
are their own, as are the toilets
of a great railway terminal
and the sequins of a very small,
very fat eyelid.
                  I take this
for myself, and you take up
the thread of my life between your teeth,
tin thread and tarnished with abuse,
you still shall hear
as long as the beast in me maintains
its taciturn power to close my lids
in tears, and my loins move yet
in the ennobling pursuit of all the worlds
you have left me alone in, and would be
the dolorous distraction from,
while you summon your army of anguishes
which is a million hooting blood vessels
on the eyes and in the ears
at that instant before death.
                     And
the menials who surrounded him critically,
languorously waiting for a
final impertinence to rebel
and enslave him, starlets and other
glittering things in the hog-wallow,
lunging mireward in their inane
mothlike adoration of niggardly
cares and stagnant respects

paid themselves, you spared,
as a hospital preserves its orderlies.
Are these your latter-day saints,
these unctuous starers, muscular
somnambulists, these stages for which
no word's been written hollow
enough, these exhibitionists in
well-veiled booths, these navel-suckers?

Is it true that you high ones, celebrated
among amorous flies, hated the
prodigy and invention of his nerves?
To withhold your light
from painstaking paths!
your love
should be difficult, as his was hard.

Nostrils of pain down avenues
of luminous spit-globes breathe in
the fragrance of his innocent flesh
like smoke, the temporary lift,
the post-cancer excitement
of vile manners and veal-thin lips,
obscure in the carelessness of your scissors.

Men cry from the grave while they still live
and now I am this dead man's voice,
stammering, a little in the earth.
I take up
the nourishment of his pale green eyes,
out of which I shall prevent
flowers from growing, your flowers.

MY HEART

I'm not going to cry all the time
nor shall I laugh all the time,
I don't prefer one "strain" to another.
I'd have the immediacy of a bad movie,
not just a sleeper, but also the big,
overproduced first-run kind. I want to be
at least as alive as the vulgar. And if
some aficionado of my mess says "That's
not like Frank!", all to the good! I
don't wear brown and grey suits all the time,
do I? No. I wear workshirts to the opera,
often. I want my feet to be bare,
I want my face to be shaven, and my heart—
you can't plan on the heart, but
the better part of it, my poetry, is open.

TO THE FILM INDUSTRY IN CRISIS

Not you, lean quarterlies and swarthy periodicals
with your studious incursions toward the pomposity of ants,
nor you, experimental theatre in which Emotive Fruition
is wedding Poetic Insight perpetually, nor you,
promenading Grand Opera, obvious as an ear (though you
are close to my heart), but you, Motion Picture Industry,
it's you I love!

In times of crisis, we must all decide again and again whom we love.
And give credit where it's due: not to my starched nurse, who taught me

how to be bad and not bad rather than good (and has lately availed
herself of this information), not to the Catholic Church
which is at best an oversolemn introduction to cosmic entertainment,
not to the American Legion, which hates everybody, but to you,
glorious Silver Screen, tragic Technicolor, amorous Cinemascope,
stretching Vistavision and startling Stereophonic Sound, with all
your heavenly dimensions and reverberations and iconoclasms! To
Richard Barthelmess as the "tol'able" boy barefoot and in pants,
Jeanette MacDonald of the flaming hair and lips and long, long neck,
Sue Carroll as she sits for eternity on the damaged fender of a car
and smiles, Ginger Rogers with her pageboy bob like a sausage
on her shuffling shoulders, peach-melba-voiced Fred Astaire of the feet,
Eric von Stroheim, the seducer of mountain-climbers' gasping spouses,
the Tarzans, each and every one of you (I cannot bring myself to prefer
Johnny Weissmuller to Lex Barker, I cannot!), Mae West in a furry sled,
her bordello radiance and bland remarks, Rudolph Valentino of the moon,
its crushing passions, and moonlike, too, the gentle Norma Shearer,
Miriam Hopkins dropping her champagne glass off Joel McCrea's yacht
and crying into the dappled sea, Clark Gable rescuing Gene Tierney
from Russia and Allan Jones rescuing Kitty Carlisle from Harpo Marx,
Cornel Wilde coughing blood on the piano keys while Merle Oberon berates,
Marilyn Monroe in her little spike heels reeling through Niagara Falls,
Joseph Cotten puzzling and Orson Welles puzzled and Dolores del Rio
eating orchids for lunch and breaking mirrors, Gloria Swanson reclining,
and Jean Harlow reclining and wiggling, and Alice Faye reclining
and wiggling and singing, Myrna Loy being calm and wise, William Powell
in his stunning urbanity, Elizabeth Taylor blossoming, yes, to you

and to all you others, the great, the near-great, the featured, the extras
who pass quickly and return in dreams saying your one or two lines,
my love!
Long may you illumine space with your marvellous appearances, delays
and enunciations, and may the money of the world glitteringly cover you
as you rest after a long day under the kleig lights with your faces
in packs for our edification, the way the clouds come often at night
but the heavens operate on the star system. It is a divine precedent
you perpetuate! Roll on, reels of celluloid, as the great earth rolls on!

ON SEEING LARRY RIVERS'
WASHINGTON CROSSING THE DELAWARE
AT THE MUSEUM OF MODERN ART

Now that our hero has come back to us
in his white pants and we know his nose
trembling like a flag under fire,
we see the calm cold river is supporting
our forces, the beautiful history.

To be more revolutionary than a nun
is our desire, to be secular and intimate
as, when sighting a redcoat, you smile
and pull the trigger. Anxieties
and animosities, flaming and feeding

on theoretical considerations and
the jealous spiritualities of the abstract,
the robot? they're smoke, billows above
the physical event. They have burned up.
See how free we are! as a nation of persons.

Dear father of our country, so alive
you must have lied incessantly to be
immediate, here are your bones crossed
on my breast like a rusty flintlock,
a pirate's flag, bravely specific

and ever so light in the misty glare
of a crossing by water in winter to a shore
other than that the bridge reaches for.
Don't shoot until, the white of freedom glinting
on your gun barrel, you see the general fear.

RADIO

Why do you play such dreary music
on Saturday afternoon, when tired
mortally tired I long for a little
reminder of immortal energy?
                                        All
week long while I trudge fatiguingly
from desk to desk in the museum
you spill your miracles of Grieg
and Honegger on shut-ins.
                                        Am I not
shut in too, and after a week
of work don't I deserve Prokofieff?

Well, I have my beautiful de Kooning
to aspire to. I think it has an orange
bed in it, more than the ear can hold.

SLEEPING ON THE WING

Perhaps it is to avoid some great sadness,
as in a Restoration tragedy the hero cries "Sleep!
O for a long sound sleep and so forget it!"
that one flies, soaring above the shoreless city,
veering upward from the pavement as a pigeon
does when a car honks or a door slams, the door
of dreams, life perpetuated in parti-colored loves
and beautiful lies all in different languages.

Fear drops away too, like the cement, and you
are over the Atlantic. Where is Spain? where is
who? The Civil War was fought to free the slaves,
was it? A sudden down-draught reminds you of gravity
and your position in respect to human love. But
here is where the gods are, speculating, bemused.
Once you are helpless, you are free, can you believe
that? Never to waken to the sad struggle of a face?
to travel always over some impersonal vastness,
to be out of, forever, neither in nor for!

The eyes roll asleep as if turned by the wind
and the lids flutter open slightly like a wing.
The world is an iceberg, so much is invisible!
and was and is, and yet the form, it may be sleeping
too. Those features etched in the ice of someone
loved who died, you are a sculptor dreaming of space
and speed, your hand alone could have done this.
Curiosity, the passionate hand of desire. Dead,
or sleeping? Is there speed enough? And, swooping,
you relinquish all that you have made your own,
the kingdom of your self sailing, for you must awake
and breathe your warmth in this beloved image
whether it's dead or merely disappearing,
as space is disappearing and your singularity.

POEM

*"Two communities outside Birmingham, Alabama, are
still searching for their dead."*   —*News Telecast*

And tomorrow morning at 8 o'clock in Springfield, Massachusetts,
my oldest aunt will be buried from a convent.

Spring is here and I am staying here, I'm not going.
Do birds fly? I am thinking my own thoughts, who else's?

    When I die, don't come, I wouldn't want a leaf
    to turn away from the sun—it loves it there.
    There's nothing so spiritual about being happy
    but you can't miss a day of it, because it doesn't last.

So this is the devil's dance? Well I was born to dance.
It's a sacred duty, like being in love with an ape,
and eventually I'll reach some great conclusion, like assumption,
when at last I meet exhaustion in these flowers, go straight up.

POEM

    Instant coffee with slightly sour cream
    in it, and a phone call to the beyond
    which doesn't seem to be coming any nearer.
    "Ah daddy, I wanna stay drunk many days"
    on the poetry of a new friend
    my life held precariously in the seeing
    hands of others, their and my impossibilities.
    Is this love, now that the first love
    has finally died, where there were no impossibilities?

IN MEMORY OF MY FEELINGS

To Grace Hartigan

I

My quietness has a man in it, he is transparent
and he carries me quietly, like a gondola, through the streets.
He has several likenesses, like stars and years, like numerals.

My quietness has a number of naked selves,
so many pistols I have borrowed to protect myselves
from creatures who too readily recognize my weapons
and have murder in their heart!
                                        though in winter
they are warm as roses, in the desert
taste of chilled anisette.
                              At times, withdrawn,
I rise into the cool skies
and gaze on at the imponderable world with the simple identification
of my colleagues, the mountains. Manfred climbs to my nape,
speaks, but I do not hear him,
                                  I'm too blue.
An elephant takes up his trumpet,
money flutters from the windows of cries, silk stretching its mirror
across shoulder blades. A gun is "fired."
                                        One of me rushes
to window #13 and one of me raises his whip and one of me
flutters up from the center of the track amidst the pink flamingoes,
and underneath their hooves as they round the last turn my lips
are scarred and brown, brushed by tails, masked in dirt's lust,
definition, open mouths gasping for the cries of the bettors for the lungs
of earth.
          So many of my transparencies could not resist the race!
Terror in earth, dried mushrooms, pink feathers, tickets,
a flaking moon drifting across the muddied teeth,
the imperceptible moan of covered breathing,
                                        love of the serpent!
I am underneath its leaves as the hunter crackles and pants
and bursts, as the barrage balloon drifts behind a cloud

and animal death whips out its flashlight,
                                        whistling
and slipping the glove off the trigger hand. The serpent's eyes
redden at sight of those thorny fingernails, he is so smooth!
                                        My transparent selves
flail about like vipers in a pail, writhing and hissing
without panic, with a certain justice of response
and presently the aquiline serpent comes to resemble the Medusa.

2
The dead hunting
and the alive, ahunted.
                        My father, my uncle,
my grand-uncle and the several aunts. My
grand-aunt dying for me, like a talisman, in the war,
before I had even gone to Borneo
her blood vessels rushed to the surface
and burst like rockets over the wrinkled
invasion of the Australians, her eyes aslant
like the invaded, but blue like mine.
An atmosphere of supreme lucidity,
                        humanism,
the mere existence of emphasis,
                                a rusted barge
painted orange against the sea
full of Marines reciting the Arabian ideas
which are a proof in themselves of seasickness
which is a proof in itself of being hunted.
A hit? *ergo* swim.
                        My 10   my 19,
my 9,   and the several years. My
12 years since they all died, philosophically speaking.
And now the coolness of a mind
like a shuttered suite in the Grand Hotel
where mail arrives for my incognito,
                                whose façade
has been slipping into the Grand Canal for centuries;
rockets splay over a *sposalizio*,

                              fleeing into night
from their Chinese memories, and it is a celebration,
the trying desperately to count them as they die.
But who will stay to be these numbers
when all the lights are dead?

3
The most arid stretch is often richest,
the hand lifting towards a fig tree from hunger
                                        digging
and there is water, clear, supple, or there
deep in the sand where death sleeps, a murmurous bubbling
proclaims the blackness that will ease and burn.
You preferred the Arabs? but they didn't stay to count
their inventions, racing into sands, converting themselves into
so many,
            embracing, at Ramadan, the tenderest effigies of
themselves with penises shorn by the hundreds, like a camel
ravishing a goat.
                    And the mountainous-minded Greeks could speak
of time as a river and step across it into Persia, leaving the pain
at home to be converted into statuary. I adore the Roman copies.
And the stench of the camel's spit I swallow,
and the stench of the whole goat. For we have advanced, France,
together into a new land, like the Greeks, where one feels nostalgic
for mere ideas, where truth lies on its deathbed like an uncle
and one of me has a sentimental longing for number,
as has another for the ball gowns of the Directoire and yet
another for "Destiny, Paris, destiny!"
                              or "Only a king may kill a king."

How many selves are there in a war hero asleep in names? under
a blanket of platoon and fleet, orderly. For every seaman
with one eye closed in fear and twitching arm at a sigh for Lord Nelson,
he is all dead; and now a meek subaltern writhes in his bedclothes
with the fury of a thousand, violating an insane mistress
who has only herself to offer his multitudes.
                              Rising,
he wraps himself in the burnoose of memories against the heat of life

and over the sands he goes to take an algebraic position *in re*
a sun of fear shining not too bravely. He will ask himselves to
vote on fear before he feels a tremor,
                              as runners arrive from the mountains
bearing snow, proof that the mind's obsolescence is still capable
of intimacy. His mistress will follow him across the desert
like a goat, towards a mirage which is something familiar about
one of his innumerable wrists,
                              and lying in an oasis one day,
playing catch with coconuts, they suddenly smell oil.

4
Beneath these lives
the ardent lover of history hides,
                              tongue out
leaving a globe of spit on a taut spear of grass
and leaves off rattling his tail a moment
to admire this flag.
                    I'm looking for my Shanghai Lil.
Five years ago, enamored of fire-escapes, I went to Chicago,
an eventful trip: the fountains! the Art Institute, the Y
for both sexes, absent Christianity.
                              At 7, before Jane
was up, the copper lake stirred against the sides
of a Norwegian freighter; on the deck a few dirty men,
tired of night, watched themselves in the water
as years before the German prisoners on the *Prinz Eugen*
dappled the Pacific with their sores, painted purple
by a Naval doctor.
                    Beards growing, and the constant anxiety
over looks. I'll shave before she wakes up. Sam Goldwyn
spent $2,000,000 on Anna Sten, but Grushenka left America.
One of me is standing in the waves, an ocean bather,
or I am naked with a plate of devils at my hip.
                                        Grace
to be born and live as variously as possible. The conception
of the masque barely suggests the sordid identifications.
I am a Hittite in love with a horse. I don't know what blood's

in me I feel like an African prince I am a girl walking downstairs
in a red pleated dress with heels I am a champion taking a fall
I am a jockey with a sprained ass-hole I am the light mist
                                        in which a face appears
and it is another face of blonde I am a baboon eating a banana
I am a dictator looking at his wife I am a doctor eating a child
and the child's mother smiling I am a Chinaman climbing a mountain
I am a child smelling his father's underwear I am an Indian
sleeping on a scalp
                and my pony is stamping in the birches,
and I've just caught sight of the *Niña,* the *Pinta* and the *Santa Maria.*
                What land is this, so free?
                                        I watch
the sea at the back of my eyes, near the spot where I think
in solitude as pine trees groan and support the enormous winds,
they are humming *L'Oiseau de feu!*
                        They look like gods, these whitemen,
and they are bringing me the horse I fell in love with on the frieze.

5
And now it is the serpent's turn.
I am not quite you, but almost, the opposite of visionary.
You are coiled around the central figure,
                                the heart
that bubbles with red ghosts, since to move is to love
and the scrutiny of all things is syllogistic,
the startled eyes of the dikdik, the bush full of white flags
fleeing a hunter,
                which is our democracy
                                but the prey
is always fragile and like something, as a seashell can be
a great Courbet, if it wishes. To bend the ear of the outer world.

                        When you turn your head
can you feel your heels, undulating? that's what it is
to be a serpent. I haven't told you of the most beautiful things
in my lives, and watching the ripple of their loss disappear
along the shore, underneath ferns,
                        face downward in the ferns

my body, the naked host to my many selves, shot
by a guerrilla warrior or dumped from a car into ferns
which are themselves *journalières.*

                          The hero, trying to unhitch his parachute,
stumbles over me. It is our last embrace.

                          And yet
I have forgotten my loves, and chiefly that one, the cancerous
statue which my body could no longer contain,

                                        against my will
                                        against my love

become art,

                          I could not change it into history
and so remember it,

                          and I have lost what is always and everywhere
present, the scene of my selves, the occasion of these ruses,
which I myself and singly must now kill

                          and save the serpent in their midst.

A STEP AWAY FROM THEM

        It's my lunch hour, so I go
        for a walk among the hum-colored
        cabs. First, down the sidewalk
        where laborers feed their dirty
        glistening torsos sandwiches
        and Coca-Cola, with yellow helmets
        on. They protect them from falling
        bricks, I guess. Then onto the
        avenue where skirts are flipping
        above heels and blow up over
        grates. The sun is hot, but the

cabs stir up the air. I look
at bargains in wristwatches. There
are cats playing in sawdust.
                    On
to Times Square, where the sign
blows smoke over my head, and higher
the waterfall pours lightly. A
Negro stands in a doorway with a
toothpick, languorously agitating.
A blonde chorus girl clicks: he
smiles and rubs his chin. Everything
suddenly honks: it is 12:40 of
a Thursday.
            Neon in daylight is a
great pleasure, as Edwin Denby would
write, as are light bulbs in daylight.
I stop for a cheeseburger at JULIET'S
CORNER. Giulietta Masina, wife of
Federico Fellini, *è bell' attrice.*
And chocolate malted. A lady in
foxes on such a day puts her poodle
in a cab.
          There are several Puerto
Ricans on the avenue today, which
makes it beautiful and warm. First
Bunny died, then John Latouche,
then Jackson Pollock. But is the
earth as full as life was full, of them?
And one has eaten and one walks,
past the magazines with nudes
and the posters for BULLFIGHT and
the Manhattan Storage Warehouse,
which they'll soon tear down. I
used to think they had the Armory
Show there.
            A glass of papaya juice
and back to work. My heart is in my
pocket, it is Poems by Pierre Reverdy.

WHY I AM NOT A PAINTER

I am not a painter, I am a poet.
Why? I think I would rather be
a painter, but I am not. Well,

for instance, Mike Goldberg
is starting a painting. I drop in.
"Sit down and have a drink" he
says. I drink; we drink. I look
up. "You have SARDINES in it."
"Yes, it needed something there."
"Oh." I go and the days go by
and I drop in again. The painting
is going on, and I go, and the days
go by. I drop in. The painting is
finished. "Where's SARDINES?"
All that's left is just
letters, "It was too much," Mike says.

But me? One day I am thinking of
a color: orange. I write a line
about orange. Pretty soon it is a
whole page of words, not lines.
Then another page. There should be
so much more, not of orange, of
words, of how terrible orange is
and life. Days go by. It is even in
prose, I am a real poet. My poem
is finished and I haven't mentioned
orange yet. It's twelve poems, I call
it ORANGES. And one day in a gallery
I see Mike's painting, called SARDINES.

POEM READ AT JOAN MITCHELL'S

At last you are tired of being single
the effort to be new does not upset you nor the effort to be other
you are not tired of life together

city noises are louder because you are together
being together you are louder than calling separately across a tele-
            phone one to the other
and there is no noise like the rare silence when you both sleep
even country noises—a dog bays at the moon, but when it loves the
            moon it bows, and the hitherto frowning moon fawns and slips

Only you in New York are not boring tonight
it is most modern to affirm some one
(we don't really love ideas, do we?)
and Joan was surprising you with a party for which I was the decoy
but you were surprising us by getting married and going away
so I am here reading poetry anyway
and no one will be bored tonight by me because you're here

Yesterday I felt very tired from being at the FIVE SPOT
and today I felt very tired from going to bed early and reading ULYSSES
but tonight I feel energetic because I'm sort of the bugle,
like waking people up, of your peculiar desire to get married

It's so
original, hydrogenic, anthropomorphic, fiscal, post-anti-esthetic,
            bland, unpicturesque and WilliamCarlosWilliamsian!
it's definitely not 19th Century, it's not even Partisan Review, it's
            new, it must be vanguard!

Tonight you probably walked over here from Bethune Street
down Greenwich Avenue with its sneaky little bars and the Women's De-
            tention House,

across 8th Street, by the acres of books and pillows and shoes and
          illuminating lampshades,
past Cooper Union where we heard the piece by Mortie Feldman with "The
          Stars and Stripes Forever" in it
and the Sagamore's terrific "coffee and, Andy," meaning "with a cheese
          Danish"—
did you spit on your index fingers and rub the CEDAR's neon circle for
          luck?
did you give a kind thought, hurrying, to Alger Hiss?

It's the day before February 17th
it is not snowing yet but it is dark and may snow yet
dreary February of the exhaustion from parties and the exceptional de-
          sire for spring which the ballet alone, by extending its run,
          has made bearable, dear New York City Ballet company, you are
          quite a bit like a wedding yourself!
and the only signs of spring are Maria Tallchief's rhinestones and a
          perky little dog barking in a bar, here and there eyes which
          suddenly light up with blue, like a ripple subsiding under a
          lily pad, or with brown, like a freshly plowed field we vow
          we'll drive out and look at when a certain Sunday comes in May—
and these eyes are undoubtedly Jane's and Joe's because they are ad-
          vancing into spring before us and tomorrow is Sunday

This poem goes on too long because our friendship has been long, long
          for this life and these times, long as art is long and un-
          interruptable,
and I would make it as long as I hope our friendship lasts if I could
          make poems that long

I hope there will be more
more drives to Bear Mountain and searches for hamburgers, more evenings
          avoiding the latest Japanese movie and watching Helen Vinson
          and Warner Baxter in *Vogues of 1938* instead, more discussions
          in lobbies of the respective greatnesses of Diana Adams and
          Allegra Kent,
more sunburns and more half-mile swims in which Joe beats me as Jane
          watches, lotion-covered and sleepy, more arguments over

Faulkner's inferiority to Tolstoy while sand gets into my
        bathing trunks
let's advance and change everything, but leave these little oases in
        case the heart gets thirsty en route
and I should probably propose myself as a godfather if you have any
        children, since I will probably earn more money some day
        accidentally, and could teach him or her how to swim
and now there is a Glazunov symphony on the radio and I think of our
        friends who are not here, of John and the nuptial quality
        of his verses (he is always marrying the whole world) and
        Janice and Kenneth, smiling and laughing, respectively (they
        are probably laughing at the Leaning Tower right now)
but we are all here and have their proxy
if Kenneth were writing this he would point out how art has changed
        women and women have changed art and men, but men haven't
        changed women much
but ideas are obscure and nothing should be obscure tonight
you will live half the year in a house by the sea and half the year in
        a house in our arms
we peer into the future and see you happy and hope it is a sign that we
        will be happy too, something to cling to, happiness
the least and best of human attainments

JOHN BUTTON BIRTHDAY

Sentiments are nice, "The Lonely Crowd,"
a rift in the clouds appears above the purple,
you find a birthday greeting card with violets
which says "a perfect friend" and means
"I love you" but the customer is forced to be
shy. It says less, as all things must.

                              But
grease sticks to the red ribs shaped like a
sea shell, grease, light and rosy that smells of
sandalwood: it's memory! I remember JA
staggering over to me in the San Remo and murmuring
"I've met someone MARVELLOUS!" That's friendship
for you, and the sentiment of introduction.

And now that I have finished dinner I can continue.

What is it that attracts one to one? Mystery?
I think of you in Paris with a red beard,
a theological student; in London talking to a friend
who lunched with Dowager Queen Mary and offered
her his last cigarette; in Los Angeles shopping
at the Supermarket; on Mount Shasta, looking . . .
above all on Mount Shasta in your unknown youth
and photograph.
                    And then the way you straighten
people out. How ambitious you are! And that you're
a painter is a great satisfaction, too. You know how
I feel about painters. I sometimes think poetry
only describes.
                    Now I have taken down the underwear
I washed last night from the various light fixtures
and can proceed.
                    And the lift of our experiences
together, which seem to me legendary. The long subways
to our old neighborhood the near East 49th and 53rd,
and before them the laughing in bars till we cried,
and the crying in movies till we laughed, the tenting
tonight on the old camp grounds! How beautiful it is
to visit someone for instant coffee! and you visiting
Cambridge, Massachusetts, talking for two weeks worth
in hours, and watching Maria Tallchief in the Public
Gardens while the swan-boats slumbered. And now,
not that I'm interrupting again, I mean your now,
you are 82 and I am 03. And in 1984 I trust we'll still

be high together. I'll say "Let's go to a bar"
and you'll say "Let's go to a movie" and we'll go to both;
like two old Chinese drunkards arguing about their
favorite mountain and the million reasons for them both.

ANXIETY

I'm having a real day of it.
                         There was
something I had to do. But what?
There are no alternatives, just
the one something.
                         I have a drink,
it doesn't help—far from it!
                         I
feel worse. I can't remember how
I felt, so perhaps I feel better.
No. Just a little darker.
                         If I could
get really dark, richly dark, like
being drunk, that's the best that's
open as a field. Not the best,

but the best except for the impossible
pure light, to be as if above a vast
prairie, rushing and pausing over
the tiny golden heads in deep grass.

But still now, familiar laughter low
from a dark face, affection human and often even—

motivational? the warm walking night
                                        wandering
amusement of darkness, lips,
                              and
the light, always in wind. Perhaps
that's it: to clean something. A window?

CAPTAIN BADA

Yes, a long cool vindt is pacing over the plains and beside it Captain
        Bada struts, shouting Hup! 1 2 3 4 like an elephant with hot nuts

it is the Captain's way of praising the sky (ja, das meer ist blau, so blau)
        into which his kepi gently pokes as he lumbers along under his baton

in the season of perennial marching. Even on 5th Avenue in États-Unis, they
        march in March, but lo! it is May already and the Captain's in his

cocky-shorts, as the sweaty breeze his hairy chest which is as dense with
        curly black and stubby grey-green greasy hairs as a certain portion

of the veldt where even the zebras are slowed down in their perennial
        chasing of each other. Speaking of perenniality, Captain Bada thinks

of the day he saw the zebras fucking. "Much more powerful than a Picabia,"
        he thinks, "with that big black piston plunging and exuding from

the distended grin of its loved one's O," and blushes at the soldiers who
        are grinning at him because of a certain other baton he has unthinkingly

grabbed before it gets tangled in a nearby tree they are being marched past.
        No privacy in the Army! but then, it is the life Captain Bada loves

as he loves his kepi and his cock and they love him. The swarthy face of CB
  wrinkles with zebraic openness and energy as he thinks, "P for Possession."

TO HELL WITH IT

"Hungry winter, this winter"
                              meaningful hints at dismay
                              to be touched, to see labeled as such
perspicacious Colette and Vladimirovitch meet with sickness and distress,

      it is because of sunspots on the sun.
                                        I clean it off with an old sock
and go on:

      And blonde Gregory dead in Fall Out on a Highway with his Broadway wife,
the last of the Lafayettes,
                              (How I hate subject matter! melancholy,
      intruding on the vigorous heart,
                                        the soul telling itself
you haven't suffered enough ((Hyalomiel))
                                        and all things that don't change,
photographs,
            monuments,
                        memories of Bunny and Gregory and me in costume
bowing to each other and the audience, like jinxes)

      nothing now can be changed, as if
                                        last crying no tears will dry
and Bunny never change her writing of
                              the Bear, nor Gregory bear me

any gift further, beyond liking my poems

                                  (no new poems for him.) and

a large red railroad handkerchief from the country

                                  in his sportscar

so like another actor:

For sentiment is always intruding on form,

                                the immaculate disgust of the mind

beaten down by pain and the vileness of life's flickering disapproval,

                  endless torment pretending to be the rose

of acknowledgement (courage)

                        and fruitless absolution (hence the word: "hip")

to be cool,

        decisive,

           precise,

                yes, while the barn door hits you in the face

each time you get up

                because the wind, seeing you slim and gallant, rises

        to embrace its darling poet. It thinks I'm mysterious.

All diseases are exchangeable.

        Wind, you'll have a terrible time
        smothering my clarity, a void
        behind my eyes,
                into which existence
        continues to stuff its wounded limbs

        as I make room for them on one
        after another filthy page of poetry.

A YOUNG POET

full of passion and giggles
                brashly erects his first poems
and they are ecstatic
             followed by a clap of praise
                          from a very few hands
belonging to other poets.
               He is sent! and they are moved to believe, once
more, freshly
        in the divine trap.
                  Two years later he has possessed
his beautiful style,
            the meaning of which draws him further down
into passion
        and up in the staring regard of his intuitions.
                           He stays up
three days in a row,
          works "morning, noon and night"
                       and then towards dawn
strolls out into the street
          to look at City Hall
              and
feel the noise of art abate
        in the silence of life.
               He is tired,
hysterical,
      he is jeered at by thugs
             and taken for a junky or a pervert
by police
    who follow him,
              as he should be followed, but not by them. He
has started his little
        magazine, and plans a city issue
                   although he's scared
to death.

Where is the castle he should inhabit on a promontory
while
        his elegies are dictated to him by the divine prosecutor?
                                                        It is
a bank on 14th Street.
                While we are seeing *The Curse of Frankenstein* he
sits in
        the 42nd Street Library, reading about the Sumerians.
                                                The threats
of inferiors are frightening
                        if you are a Negro choosing your own High School,
or a painter too drunk
                to fight off a mugging,
                                        or a poet exhausted by
the insight which comes as a kiss
                        and follows as a curse.

ODE ON NECROPHILIA

"Isn't there any body you want back from
the grave? We were less generous in our time."
        —*Palinurus* (not *Cyril Connolly*)

Well,
        it is better
                that

                                O M E O N
                        S love them E

        and we
                so seldom look on love
                                that it seems heinous

122

POEM

To be idiomatic in a vacuum,
it is a shining thing! I

see it, it's like being inside
a bird. Where do you live,

are you sick?
I am breathing the pure sphere

of loneliness and it is sating.
Do you know young René Rilke?

He is a rose, he is together, all
together, like a wind tunnel,

and the rest of us are testing
our wings, our straining struts.

ODE TO MICHAEL GOLDBERG ('S BIRTH AND OTHER BIRTHS)

I don't remember anything of then, down there around the magnolias
        where I was no more comfortable than I've been since
        though aware of a certain neutrality called satisfaction
        sometimes

and there's never been an opportunity to think of it as an idyll
as if everyone'd been singing around me, or around a tulip tree

a faint stirring of that singing seems to come to me in heavy traffic
but I can't be sure that's it, it may be some more recent singing
from hours of dusk in bushes playing tag, being called in, walking
       up onto the porch crying bitterly because it wasn't a veranda
"smell that honeysuckle?" or a door you can see through terribly clearly,
          even the mosquitoes saw through it
suffocating netting
or more often being put into a brown velvet suit and kicked around
perhaps that was my last real cry for myself
in a forest you think of birds, in traffic you think of tires,
       where are you?
in Baltimore you think of hats and shoes, like Daddy did

              I hardly ever think of June 27, 1926
              when I came moaning into my mother's world
              and tried to make it mine immediately
              by screaming, sucking, urinating
              and carrying on generally
              it was quite a day

I wasn't proud of my penis yet, how did I know how to act? it was 1936
"no excuses, now"

      Yellow morning
              silent, wet
                    blackness under the trees over stone walls
hay, smelling faintly of semen
                a few sheltered flowers nodding and smiling
at the clattering cutter-bar
                of the mower ridden by Jimmy Whitney
"I'd like to put my rolling-pin to her"   his brother Bailey
leaning on his pitchfork, watching
                "you shove it in and nine months later
it comes out a kid"
            Ha ha   where those flowers would dry out
and never again be seen
            except as cow-flaps, hushed noon drinking cold

water in the dusty field   "their curly throats"   big milk cans

          full of cold spring water, sandy hair, black hair

                    I went to my first movie
                    and the hero got his legs
                    cut off by a steam engine
                    in a freightyard, in my second

                    Karen Morley got shot
                    in the back by an arrow
                    I think she was an heiress
                    it came through her bathroom door

                    there was nobody there
                    there never was anybody
                    there at any time
                    in sweet-smelling summer

I'd like to stay

                    in this field forever

                                        and think of nothing

but these sounds,

                    these smells and the tickling grasses
                                        "up your ass, Sport"

                    Up on the mountainous hill
                    behind the confusing house
                    where I lived, I went each
                    day after school and some nights
                    with my various dogs, the
                    terrier that bit people, Arno
                    the shepherd (who used to
                    be wild but had stopped), the
                    wire-haired that took fits
                    and finally the boring gentle
                    cocker, spotted brown and white,
                    named Freckles   there,

the wind sounded exactly like
Stravinsky
                I first recognized art
as wildness, and it seemed right,
                I mean rite, to me

climbing the water tower I'd
look out for hours in wind
and the world seemed rounder
and fiercer and I was happier
because I wasn't scared of falling off

nor off the horses, the horses!
to hell with the horses, bay and black

It's odd to have secrets at an early age, trysts
whose thoughtfulness and sweetness are those of a very aggressive person
                carried beneath your shirt like an amulet against your sire
                what one must do is done in a red twilight
                        on colossally old and dirty furniture with knobs,
                and on Sunday afternoons you meet in a high place
                watching the Sunday drivers and the symphonic sadness
                stopped, a man in a convertible put his hand up a girl's skirt
        and again the twitching odor of hay, like a minor irritation
that gives you a hardon, and again the roundness of horse noises

                "Je suis las de vivre au pays natal"
                        but unhappiness, like Mercury, transfixed me
                there, un repaire de vipères
                        and had I known the strength and durability
of those invisible bonds I would have leaped from rafters onto prongs
then
                and been carried shining and intact
                to the Indian Cemetery near the lake

                                        but there is a glistening
                                        blackness in the center
                                        if you seek it

126

here . . .   it's capable of bursting
                 into flame or merely
                 gleaming profoundly in

                                   the platinum setting
                                   of your ornamental
                                   human ties and hates

hanging between breasts
                      or, crosslike, on a chest of hairs
the center of myself is never silent
                                  the wind soars, keening overhead
and the vestments of unnatural safety
                                 part to reveal a foreign land
toward whom I have been selected to bear
                                 the gift of fire
                 the temporary place of light, the land of air

down where a flame illumines gravity and means warmth and insight,
       where air is flesh, where speed is darkness
and
       things can suddenly be reached, held, dropped and known

where a not totally imaginary ascent can begin all over again in tears

              A couple of specifically anguished days
              make me now distrust sorrow, simple sorrow
              especially, like sorrow over death

              it makes you wonder who you are to be sorrowful
              over death, death belonging to another
              and suddenly inhabited by you without permission

              you moved in impulsively and took it up
              declaring your Squatters' Rights in howls
              or screaming with rage, like a parvenu in a Chinese laundry

              disbelieving your own feelings is the worst
              and you suspect that you are jealous of this death

YIPPEE! I'm glad I'm alive
                              "I'm glad you're alive
         too, baby, because I want to fuck you"
                                        you are pink
         and despicable in the warm breeze drifting in the window
and the rent
              is due, in honor of which you have borrowed $34.96 from Joe
and it's all over but the smoldering hatred of pleasure
         a gorgeous purple like somebody's favorite tie
              "Shit, that means you're getting kind of ascetic, doesn't it?"

                    So I left, the stars were shining
                    like the lights around a swimming pool

                    you've seen a lot of anemones, too
                    haven't you, Old Paint? through the
                    Painted Desert to the orange covered
                    slopes where a big hill was moving in
                    on L A and other stars were strolling
                    in shorts down palm-stacked horse-walks
                    and I stared with my strained SP stare
                    wearing a gun
                              the doubts
         of a life devoted to leaving rumors of love for new
from does she love me to do I love him,
                              sempiternal farewell to hearths
and the gods who don't live there

                    in New Guinea a Sunday morning figure
                    reclining outside his hut in Lamourish languor
                    and an atabrine-dyed hat like a sick sun
                    over his ebony land on your way to breakfast

                    he has had his balls sewed into his mouth
                    by the natives who bleach their hair in urine
                    and their will; a basketball game and a concert
                    later if you live to write, it's not all advancing
                    towards you, he had a killing desire for their women

but more killing still the absence of desire, which in religion
                              used to be called hope,
I don't just mean the lack of a hardon, which may be sincerity
                    or the last-minute victory of the proud spirit over flesh,
      no: a tangerinelike sullenness in the face of sunrise
                    or a dark sinking in the wind on the forecastle
      when someone you love hits your head and says "I'd sail with you any
                              where, war or no war"
      who was about
                    to die a tough blond death
                                             like a slender blighted palm
      in the hurricane's curious hail
                                   and the maelstrom of bulldozers
                    and metal sinkings,
                                        churning the earth
      even under the fathomless deaths
                                   below, beneath
                                             where the one special
                    went to be hidden, never to disappear
                    not spatial in that way

        Take me, I felt, into the future fear of saffron pleasures
crazy strangeness and steam
                         of seeing a (pearl) white whale, steam of
being high in the sky
                    opening fire on Corsairs,
                                        kept moving in berths
where I trade someone *The Counterfeiters* (I thought it was about personal
freedom then!) for a pint of whiskey,
                                   banana brandy in Manila, spidery
steps trailing down onto the rocks of the harbor
                                        and up in the black fir, the
pyramidal whiteness, Genji on the Ginza,
                                   a lavender-kimono-sized
loneliness,
           and drifting into my ears off Sendai in the snow Carl
T. Fischer's *Recollections of an Indian Boy*

                                        this tiny overdecorated
rock garden bringing obviously heart-shaped
                                        the Great Plains, as is
my way to be obvious as eight o'clock in the dining car
                                        of the
20th Century Limited (express)
                                and its noisy blast passing buttes to be
Atchison-Topeka-Santa Fé, Baltimore and Ohio (Cumberland),
                                        leaving
beds in Long Beach for beds in Boston, via C- (D,B,) 47 (6)
pretty girls in textile mills,
                                drowsing on bales in a warehouse of cotton
listening to soft Southern truck talk
                                perhaps it is "your miraculous
low roar" on Ulithi as the sailors pee into funnels, ambassadors of
                green-beer-interests bigger than Standard Oil in the South
Pacific, where the beaches flower with cat-eyes and ear fungus
                        warm as we never wanted to be warm, in an ammunition
dump, my foot again crushed (this time by a case of 40 millimeters)
                                                        "the
        only thing you ever gave New Guinea was your toenail and now
        the Australians are taking over"   . . . the pony of war?

                to "return" safe who will never feel safe
                and loves to ride steaming in the autumn of
                centuries of useless aspiration towards artifice
                        are you feeling useless, too, Old Paint?
                I am really an Indian at heart, knowing it is all
                all over but my own ceaseless going, never
                to be just a hill of dreams and flint for someone later
                but a hull laved by the brilliant Celebes response,
                empty of treasure to the explorers who sailed me not

King Philip's trail,
                        lachrymose highway of infantile regrets and cayuse
meannesses,
                        Mendelssohn driving me mad in Carnegie Hall like greed
grasping

Palisades Park smiling, you pull a pretty ring out of the pineapple
and blow yourself up
                              contented to be a beautiful fan of blood
                                    above the earth-empathic earth

          Now suddenly the fierce wind of disease and Venus, as
when a child
                    you wonder if you're not a little crazy, laughing
because a horse
                    is standing on your foot
                                        and you're kicking his hock
with your sneaker, which is to him
                                        a love-tap, baring big teeth
laughing . . .
                    thrilling activities which confuse
                                        too many, too loud
too often, crowds of intimacies and no distance
                                        the various cries
and rounds
                    and we are smiling in our confused way, darkly
in the back alcove
                    of the Five Spot, devouring chicken-in-the-basket
and arguing,
                    the four of us, about loyalty

                    wonderful stimulation of bitterness
                    to be young and to grow bigger
                    more and more cells, like germs
                    or a political conspiracy

                    and each reason for love always
                    a certain hostility, mistaken
                    for wisdom
                              exceptional excitement
                    which is finally simple blindness
                    (but not to be sneezed at!) like
                    a successful American satellite . . .

Yes, it does, it would still
keep me out of a monastery if
I were invited to attend one

                              from round the window, you can't
          see the street!
                    you let the cold wind course through
and let the heart pump and gurgle
                              in febrile astonishment,
                                        a cruel world
          to which you've led it by your mind,
                              bicycling no-hands
                                        leaving it gasping
          there, wondering where you are and how to get back,
                                        although you'll never let
               it go

          while somewhere everything's dispersed
at five o'clock
          for Martinis a group of professional freshnesses meet
and the air's like a shrub—Rose o' Sharon? the others,
                                        it's not
a flickering light for us, but the glare of the dark
                                        too much endlessness
stored up, and in store:
                    "the exquisite prayer
                    to be new each day
                    brings to the artist
                    only a certain kneeness"

I am assuming that everything is all right and difficult,
                                        where hordes
          of stars carry the burdens of the gentler animals like our-
          selves with wit and austerity beneath a hazardous settlement
which we understand because we made
                                        and secretly admire
          because it moves

yes! for always, for it is our way, to pass the teahouse and the ceremony
            by and rather fall sobbing to the floor with joy and freezing
            than to spill the kid upon the table and then thank the blood

      for flowing
                        as it must throughout the miserable, clear and willful
life we love beneath the blue,
                        a fleece of pure intention sailing like
a pinto in a barque of slaves
                        who soon will turn upon their captors
lower anchor, found a city riding there
                                    of poverty and sweetness paralleled
            among the races without time,
                                    and one alone will speak of being
            born in pain
                        and he will be the wings of an extraordinary liberty

ODE (TO JOSEPH LESUEUR)
ON THE ARROW THAT FLIETH BY DAY

To humble yourself before a radio on a Sunday
it's amusing, like dying after a party
"click"/and you're dead from fall-out, hang-over
            or something hyphenated

(hello, Western Union? send a Mother's Day message to Russia: SORRY
NOT TO BE WITH YOU ON YOUR DAY LOVE AND KISSES TELL THE CZAR LA GRANDE
JATTE WASNT DAMAGED IN THE MUSEUM OF MODERN ART FIRE /S/ FRANK)

the unrecapturable nostalgia for nostalgia
for a life I might have hated, thus mourned

but do we really need anything more to be sorry about
wouldn't it be extra, as all pain is extra

(except that I will never feel CONTEST: WIN A DREAM TRIP pertains to
me, somehow   Joe, I wouldn't go, probably)

for God's sake fly the other way
leave me standing alone crumbling in the new sky of the Wide World
without passage, without breath

a spatial representative of emptiness

if Joan says I'm wounded, then I'm wounded
and not like La Pucelle or André Gide
not by moral issues or the intercontinental ballistics missile
            or the Seer of Prague

(you're right to go to Aaron's PIANO FANTASY, but I'm not up to it this
time, too important a piece not to punish me
                                    and it's raining)

it's more like the death of a nation
henceforth to be called small

although its people could say "Mare nostrum" without fear of hubris
and the air saluted them
                        (air of the stars) ashore or leaning on the prow

ODE ON CAUSALITY

There is the sense of neurotic coherence

you think maybe poetry is too important and you like that

suddenly everyone's supposed to be veined, like marble

it isn't that simple but it's simple enough

the rock is least living of the forms man has fucked

and it isn't pathetic and it's lasting, one towering tree

in the vast smile of bronze and vertiginous grasses

Maude lays down her doll, red wagon and her turtle
takes my hand and comes with us, shows the bronze JACKSON POLLOCK
gazelling on the rock of her demeanor as a child, says running
away hand in hand "he isn't under there, he's out in the woods" beyond

and like that child at your grave make me be distant and imaginative
make my lines thin as ice, then swell like pythons
the color of Aurora when she first brought fire to the Arctic in a sled
a sexual bliss inscribe upon the page of whatever energy I burn for art
and do not watch over my life, but read and read through copper earth

not to fall at all, but disappear or burn! seizing a grave by throat
which is the look of earth, its ambiguity of light and sound
the thickness in a look of lust, the air within the eye
the gasp of a moving hand as maps change and faces become vacant
it's noble to refuse to be added up or divided, finality of kings

and there's the ugliness we seek in vain
through life and long for like a mortuarian Baudelaire working for Skouras

inhabiting neighborhoods of Lear! Lear! Lear!
                       tenement of a single heart

for Old Romance was draping dolors on a scarlet mound, each face
a country of valorous decay, heath-helmet or casque, *mollement, moelleusement*
and all that shining fierce turned green and covered the lays with grass
as later in *The Orange Ballad of Cromwell's Charm Upon the Height "So Green"*
as in the histories of that same time and earlier, when written down at all
sweet scripts to obfuscate the tender subjects of their future lays

to be layed at all! romanticized, elaborated, fucked, sung, put to "rest"
is worse than the mild apprehension of a Buddhist type caught halfway up
the tea-rose trellis with his sickle banging on the Monk's lead window, moon
not our moon
           unless the tea exude a little gas and poisonous fact
to reach the spleen and give it a dreamless twinge that love's love's near

        the bang of alertness, loneliness, position that prehends experience

not much to be less, not much to be more
                   alive, sick; and dead, dying
like the kiss of love meeting the kiss of hatred
                   "oh you know why"
each in asserting beginning to be more of the opposite
                    what goes up must
come down, what dooms must do, standing still and walking in New York

let us walk in that nearby forest, staring into the growling trees
in which an era of pompous frivolity or two is dangling its knobby knees
and reaching for an audience
                 over the pillar of our deaths a cloud
heaves
     pushed, steaming and blasted
                 love-propelled and tangled glitteringly
        has earned himself the title *Bird in Flight*

ODE: SALUTE TO THE FRENCH NEGRO POETS

From near the sea, like Whitman my great predecessor, I call
to the spirits of other lands to make fecund my existence

do not spare your wrath upon our shores, that trees may grow
upon the sea, mirror of our total mankind in the weather

one who no longer remembers dancing in the heat of the moon may call
across the shifting sands, trying to live in the terrible western world

here where to love at all's to be a politician, as to love a poem
is pretentious, this may sound tendentious but it's lyrical

which shows what lyricism has been brought to by our fabled times
where cowards are shibboleths and one specific love's traduced

by shame for what you love more generally and never would avoid
where reticence is paid for by a poet in his blood or ceasing to be

blood! blood that we have mountains in our veins to stand off jackals
in the pillaging of our desires and allegiances, Aimé Césaire

for if there is fortuity it's in the love we bear each other's differences
in race which is the poetic ground on which we rear our smiles

standing in the sun of marshes as we wade slowly toward the culmination
of a gift which is categorically the most difficult relationship

and should be sought as such because it is our nature, nothing
inspires us but the love we want upon the frozen face of earth

and utter disparagement turns into praise as generations read the message
of our hearts in adolescent closets who once shot at us in doorways

or kept us from living freely because they were too young then to know
what they would ultimately need from a barren and heart-sore life

the beauty of America, neither cool jazz nor devoured Egyptian heroes, lies in
lives in the darkness I inhabit in the midst of sterile millions

the only truth is face to face, the poem whose words become your mouth
and dying in black and white we fight for what we love, not are

A TRUE ACCOUNT OF TALKING
TO THE SUN AT FIRE ISLAND

The Sun woke me this morning loud
and clear, saying "Hey! I've been
trying to wake you up for fifteen
minutes. Don't be so rude, you are
only the second poet I've ever chosen
to speak to personally
                              so why
aren't you more attentive? If I could
burn you through the window I would
to wake you up. I can't hang around
here all day."
                    "Sorry, Sun, I stayed
up late last night talking to Hal."

"When I woke up Mayakovsky he was
a lot more prompt" the Sun said
petulantly. "Most people are up
already waiting to see if I'm going

to put in an appearance."
                              I tried
to apologize "I missed you yesterday."
"That's better" he said. "I didn't
know you'd come out." "You may be
wondering why I've come so close?"
"Yes" I said beginning to feel hot
wondering if maybe he wasn't burning me
anyway.

              "Frankly I wanted to tell you
I like your poetry. I see a lot
on my rounds and you're okay. You may
not be the greatest thing on earth, but
you're different. Now, I've heard some
say you're crazy, they being excessively
calm themselves to my mind, and other
crazy poets think that you're a boring
reactionary. Not me.

                        Just keep on
like I do and pay no attention. You'll
find that people always will complain
about the atmosphere, either too hot
or too cold too bright or too dark, days
too short or too long.

                        If you don't appear
at all one day they think you're lazy
or dead. Just keep right on, I like it.

And don't worry about your lineage
poetic or natural. The Sun shines on
the jungle, you know, on the tundra
the sea, the ghetto. Wherever you were
I knew it and saw you moving. I was waiting
for you to get to work.

                        And now that you
are making your own days, so to speak,
even if no one reads you but me

you won't be depressed. Not
everyone can look up, even at me. It
hurts their eyes."
                    "Oh Sun, I'm so grateful to you!"

"Thanks and remember I'm watching. It's
easier for me to speak to you out
here. I don't have to slide down
between buildings to get your ear.
I know you love Manhattan, but
you ought to look up more often.
                                        And
always embrace things, people earth
sky stars, as I do, freely and with
the appropriate sense of space. That
is your inclination, known in the heavens
and you should follow it to hell, if
necessary, which I doubt.
                                Maybe we'll
speak again in Africa, of which I too
am specially fond. Go back to sleep now
Frank, and I may leave a tiny poem
in that brain of yours as my farewell."

"Sun, don't go!" I was awake
at last. "No, go I must, they're calling
me."
        "Who are they?"
                                Rising he said "Some
day you'll know. They're calling to you
too." Darkly he rose, and then I slept.

TO GOTTFRIED BENN

Poetry is not instruments
that work at times
then walk out on you
laugh at you old
get drunk on you young
poetry's part of your self

like the passion of a nation
at war it moves quickly
provoked to defense or aggression
unreasoning power
an instinct for self-declaration

like nations its faults are absorbed
in the heat of sides and angles
combatting the void of rounds
a solid of imperfect placement
nations get worse and worse

but not wrongly revealed
in the universal light of tragedy

HEROIC SCULPTURE

We join the animals
not when we fuck
or shit
not when tear falls

but when
staring into light
we think

THE "UNFINISHED"

In memory of Bunny Lang

As happiness takes off the tie it borrowed from me
and gets into bed and pretends to be asleep-and-awake
or pulls an orange poncho over its blonde Jay-Thorped curls
and goes off to cocktails without telling me why
it's so depressing,
so I will be as unhappy as I damn well
please and not make too much of it because I am
really here and not in a novel or anything or a jet plane
as I've often gone away on a ladder, a taxi or a jet plane

everybody thinks if you go, you go up
but I'm not so sure about that because the fault of my generation
is that nobody wants to make a big *histoire* about anything
and I'm just like everybody else, if an earthquake comes
laughingly along and gulps down the whole of Madrid
including the Manzanares River and for dessert all the royal tombs

in the Escorial I'd only get kind of hysterical about one person
no Voltaire me
                        and isn't it funny how beautiful Sibelius sounds
if you haven't found him for a long time? because if we didn't all
hang onto a little self-conscious bitterness and call it intelligence
and admire it as technique we would all be perfectly truthful
and fall into the vat of longing and suffocate in its suet
except for the two Gregorys
                                Lafayette who was so pointlessly handsome
and innocently blond that he cheerfully died
                                and Corso
too lustrously dark and precise, he would be excavated and declared
a black diamond and hung round a slender bending neck
in the 26th Century when the Court of the Bourbons is reinstated
and heaven comes to resemble more closely a late Goya

        this isn't bitterness, it's merely a tremor of the earth
I'm impersonating some wretch weeping over a 1956 date book and of course
I pull myself together and then I wipe my eyes and see that it's my own
                        (date book, that is)
and everything becomes history: when Lennie Bernstein conducted it
on TV last week he called it my Symphony Number One, my "Unfinished"
that sort of thing can give you a terrible feeling that you've
                        accomplished something

meanwhile, back at the Paris branch of contemporary depression, I
am dropping through the famous blueness like a pearl diver, I am
looking for Gregory who lives on Heart-Bed Street and I sit with Ashbery
in the Flore because of his poem about himself in a flower-bed
and we look for Gregory in the Deux Magots because I want to cry with him
about a dear dead friend, it's always about dying, never about death
I sometimes think it's the only reason that any of us love each other
it is raining, Ashes helps me finish my gall and seltzer, and we go

        the casual reader will not, I am sure, be averse to a short
        digression in this splendid narrative by which the nature
        of the narrator can be more or less revealed and all sorts
        of things subsequently become clear*er* if not clear: picture

a person who one day in a fit of idleness decides to make
a pomander like the one that granny used to have around the
house in old New England and so he takes an orange and sticks
a lot of cloves in it and then he looks at it and realizes
that he's killed the orange, his favorite which came from
the Malay Archipelago and was even loved in Ancient China,
and he quickly pulls out all the cloves, but it's too
late! Orange is lying bleeding in my hand! and I
suddenly think of the moon, hanging quietly up there
ever since the time of Keats, and now they're shoot-
ing all those funny-looking things at her, that's
what you get, baby (end of digression)

and back in New York Gregory is back in New York and we are still missing
each other in the Cedar and in hotel lobbies where Salvador Dali is
supposed to be asleep and at Anne Truxell's famous giggling parties
until one fine day (*vedremo*) we meet over a duck dinner, good god
I just remembered what he stuffed it with, you guessed it: oranges!
and perhaps, too, he is the true narrator of this story, Gregory

no, I must be, because he's in Chicago, and after all those months
including Madrid where it turns out there wasn't any earthquake
and also the TV broadcast was cancelled because Bernstein had a sore
thumb, I'm not depressed any more, because Gregory has had the same
experience with oranges, and is alive

where all memories grow into childhood
and mingled sound and silence drifts up to the rooftop
where a bare-legged boy stares into the future
takes up the knives of his wounds to catch the light
foreseeing his epic triumph in the style of Cecil B. De Mille
when one day the Via del Corso is named after him
the principal street of Rome
which is better than the Nobel Prize
better than Albert Schweitzer, Pablo Casals and Helen Keller
PUT TO GETHER

IMAGE OF THE BUDDHA PREACHING

I am very happy to be here at the Villa Hügel
and Prime Minister Nehru has asked me to greet the people of Essen
and to tell you how powerfully affected we in India
have been by Germany's philosophy, traditions and mythology
though our lucidity and our concentration on archetypes
puts us in a class by ourself
                        "for in this world of storm and stress"
—5,000 years of Indian art! just think of it, oh Essen!
is this a calmer region of thought, "a reflection of the mind
through the ages"?
                  Max Müller, "primus inter pares" among Indologists
remember our byword, Mokshamula, I rejoice in the fact of 900 exhibits

I deeply appreciate filling the gaps, oh Herr Doktor Heinrich Goetz!
and the research purring onward in Pakistan and Ceylon and Afghanistan
soapstone, terracotta-Indus, terracotta-Maurya, terracotta-Sunga,
    terracotta-Andhra, terracotta fragments famous Bharhut Stupa
Kushana, Gandhara, Gupta, Hindu and Jain, Secco, Ajanta, Villa Hügel!

Anglo-German trade will prosper by Swansea-Mannheim friendship
waning now the West Wall by virtue of two rolls per capita
and the flagship BERLIN is joining its "white fleet" on the Rhine
though better schools and model cars are wanting, still still oh Essen
    Nataraja dances on the dwarf
    and unlike their fathers
    Germany's highschool pupils love the mathematics

    which is hopeful of a new delay in terror
    I don't think

THE DAY LADY DIED

It is 12:20 in New York a Friday
three days after Bastille day, yes
it is 1959 and I go get a shoeshine
because I will get off the 4:19 in Easthampton
at 7:15 and then go straight to dinner
and I don't know the people who will feed me

I walk up the muggy street beginning to sun
and have a hamburger and a malted and buy
an ugly NEW WORLD WRITING to see what the poets
in Ghana are doing these days
                              I go on to the bank
and Miss Stillwagon (first name Linda I once heard)
doesn't even look up my balance for once in her life
and in the GOLDEN GRIFFIN I get a little Verlaine
for Patsy with drawings by Bonnard although I do
think of Hesiod, trans. Richmond Lattimore or
Brendan Behan's new play or *Le Balcon* or *Les Nègres*
of Genet, but I don't, I stick with Verlaine
after practically going to sleep with quandariness

and for Mike I just stroll into the PARK LANE
Liquor Store and ask for a bottle of Strega and
then I go back where I came from to 6th Avenue
and the tobacconist in the Ziegfeld Theatre and
casually ask for a carton of Gauloises and a carton
of Picayunes, and a NEW YORK POST with her face on it

and I am sweating a lot by now and thinking of
leaning on the john door in the 5 SPOT
while she whispered a song along the keyboard
to Mal Waldron and everyone and I stopped breathing

RHAPSODY

515 Madison Avenue
door to heaven? portal
stopped realities and eternal licentiousness
or at least the jungle of impossible eagerness
your marble is bronze and your lianas elevator cables
swinging from the myth of ascending
I would join
or declining the challenge of racial attractions
they zing on (into the lynch, dear friends)
while everywhere love is breathing draftily
like a doorway linking 53rd with 54th
the east-bound with the west-bound traffic by 8,000,000s
o midtown tunnels and the tunnels, too, of Holland

where is the summit where all aims are clear
the pin-point light upon a fear of lust
as agony's needlework grows up around the unicorn
and fences him for milk- and yoghurt-work
when I see Gianni I know he's thinking of John Ericson
playing the Rachmaninoff 2nd or Elizabeth Taylor
taking sleeping-pills and Jane thinks of Manderley
and Irkutsk while I cough lightly in the smog of desire
and my eyes water achingly imitating the true blue

a sight of Manahatta in the towering needle
multi-faceted insight of the fly in the stringless labyrinth
Canada plans a higher place than the Empire State Building
I am getting into a cab at 9th Street and 1st Avenue
and the Negro driver tells me about a $120 apartment
"where you can't walk across the floor after 10 at night
not even to pee, cause it keeps them awake downstairs"
no, I don't like that "well, I didn't take it"
perfect in the hot humid morning on my way to work
a little supper-club conversation for the mill of the gods

you were there always and you know all about these things
as indifferent as an encyclopedia with your calm brown eyes
it isn't enough to smile when you run the gauntlet
you've got to spit like Niagara Falls on everybody or
Victoria Falls or at least the beautiful urban fountains of Madrid
as the Niger joins the Gulf of Guinea near the Menemsha Bar
that is what you learn in the early morning passing Madison Avenue
where you've never spent any time and stores eat up light

I have always wanted to be near it
though the day is long (and I don't mean Madison Avenue)
lying in a hammock on St. Mark's Place sorting my poems
in the rancid nourishment of this mountainous island
they are coming and we holy ones must go
is Tibet historically a part of China? as I historically
belong to the enormous bliss of American death

SONG

Is it dirty
does it look dirty
that's what you think of in the city

does it just seem dirty
that's what you think of in the city
you don't refuse to breathe do you

someone comes along with a very bad character
he seems attractive. is he really. yes. very
he's attractive as his character is bad. is it. yes

that's what you think of in the city
run your finger along your no-moss mind
that's not a thought that's soot

and you take a lot of dirt off someone
is the character less bad. no. it improves constantly
you don't refuse to breathe do you

ADIEU TO NORMAN,
BON JOUR TO JOAN AND JEAN-PAUL

It is 12:10 in New York and I am wondering
if I will finish this in time to meet Norman for lunch
ah lunch! I think I am going crazy
what with my terrible hangover and the weekend coming up
at excitement-prone Kenneth Koch's
I wish I were staying in town and working on my poems
at Joan's studio for a new book by Grove Press
which they will probably not print
but it is good to be several floors up in the dead of night
wondering whether you are any good or not
and the only decision you can make is that you did it

yesterday I looked up the rue Frémicourt on a map
and was happy to find it like a bird
flying over Paris et ses environs
which unfortunately did not include Seine-et-Oise which I don't know
as well as a number of other things
and Allen is back talking about god a lot
and Peter is back not talking very much

and Joe has a cold and is not coming to Kenneth's
although he is coming to lunch with Norman
I suspect he is making a distinction
well, who isn't

I wish I were reeling around Paris
instead of reeling around New York
I wish I weren't reeling at all
it is Spring the ice has melted the Ricard is being poured
we are all happy and young and toothless
it is the same as old age
the only thing to do is simply continue
is that simple
yes, it is simple because it is the only thing to do
can you do it
yes, you can because it is the only thing to do
blue light over the Bois de Boulogne it continues
the Seine continues
the Louvre stays open it continues it hardly closes at all
the Bar Américain continues to be French
de Gaulle continues to be Algerian as does Camus
Shirley Goldfarb continues to be Shirley Goldfarb
and Jane Hazan continues to be Jane Freilicher (I think!)
and Irving Sandler continues to be the balayeur des artistes
and so do I (sometimes I think I'm "in love" with painting)
and surely the Piscine Deligny continues to have water in it
and the Flore continues to have tables and newspapers and people under them
and surely we shall not continue to be unhappy
we shall be happy
but we shall continue to be ourselves everything continues to be possible
René Char, Pierre Reverdy, Samuel Beckett it is possible isn't it
I love Reverdy for saying yes, though I don't believe it

JOE'S JACKET

Entraining to Southampton in the parlor car with Jap and Vincent, I
see life as a penetrable landscape lit from above
like it was in my Barbizonian kiddy days when automobiles
were owned by the same people for years and the Alfa Romeo was
only a rumor under the leaves beside the viaduct and I
pretending to be adult felt the blue within me and the light up there
no central figure me, I was some sort of cloud or a gust of wind
at the station a crowd of drunken fishermen on a picnic Kenneth
is hard to find but we find, through all the singing, Kenneth smiling
it is off to Janice's bluefish and the incessant talk of affection
expressed as excitability and spleen to be recent and strong
and not unbearably right in attitude, full of confidences
now I will say it, thank god, I knew you would

an enormous party mesmerizing comers in the disgathering light
and dancing miniature-endless, like a pivot
I drink to smother my sensitivity for a while so I won't stare away
I drink to kill the fear of boredom, the mounting panic of it
I drink to reduce my seriousness so a certain spurious charm
can appear and win its flickering little victory over noise
I drink to die a little and increase the contrast of this questionable moment
and then I am going home, purged of everything except anxiety and self-distrust
now I will say it, thank god, I knew you would
and the rain has commenced its delicate lament over the orchards

an enormous window morning and the wind, the beautiful desperation of a tree
fighting off strangulation, and my bed has an ugly calm
I reach to the D. H. Lawrence on the floor and read "The Ship of Death"
I lie back again and begin slowly to drift and then to sink
a somnolent envy of inertia makes me rise naked and go to the window
where the car horn mysteriously starts to honk, no one is there
and Kenneth comes out and stops it in the soft green lightless stare
and we are soon in the Paris of Kenneth's libretto, I did not drift
away I did not die I am there with Haussmann and the rue de Rivoli

and the spirits of beauty, art and progress, pertinent and mobile
in their worldly way, and musical and strange the sun comes out

returning by car the forceful histories of myself and Vincent loom
like the city hour after hour closer and closer to the future I am here
and the night is heavy though not warm, Joe is still up and we talk
only of the immediate present and its indiscriminately hitched-to past
the feeling of life and incident pouring over the sleeping city
which seems to be bathed in an unobtrusive light which lends things
coherence and an absolute, for just that time as four o'clock goes by

and soon I am rising for the less than average day, I have coffee
I prepare calmly to face almost everything that will come up I am calm
but not as my bed was calm as it softly declined to become a ship
I borrow Joe's seersucker jacket though he is still asleep I start out
when I last borrowed it I was leaving there it was on my Spanish plaza back
and hid my shoulders from San Marco's pigeons was jostled on the Kurfürstendamm
and sat opposite Ashes in an enormous leather chair in the Continental
it is all enormity and life it has protected me and kept me here on
many occasions as a symbol does when the heart is full and risks no speech
a precaution I loathe as the pheasant loathes the season and is preserved
it will not be need, it will be just what it is and just what happens

YOU ARE GORGEOUS AND I'M COMING

Vaguely I hear the purple roar of the torn-down Third Avenue El
it sways slightly but firmly like a hand or a golden-downed thigh
normally I don't think of sounds as colored unless I'm feeling corrupt
concrete Rimbaud obscurity of emotion which is simple and very definite
even lasting, yes it may be that dark and purifying wave, the death of boredom

nearing the heights themselves may destroy you in the pure air
to be further complicated, confused, empty but refilling, exposed to light

With the past falling away as an acceleration of nerves thundering and shaking
aims its aggregating force like the Métro towards a realm of encircling travel
rending the sound of adventure and becoming ultimately local and intimate
repeating the phrases of an old romance which is constantly renewed by the
endless originality of human loss the air the stumbling quiet of breathing
newly the heavens' stars all out we are all for the captured time of our being

SAINT

Like a pile of gold that his breath
is forming into slender columns
of various sizes, Vincent lies all
in a heap as even the sun must rest

and air and the noises of Manhattan
he thinks he is not a de Paul yet
the market is sagging today and he
doesn't mind, he is waiting for his sofa

to arrive from Toronto, that's what
he thinks and of whether Maxine
would like a pair of jet earrings
well she would, emotionally at least

and what other way is there to like
in the sea in the salt ease
he founders childlike and aggressive
until the tow draws him out

and scared he swims for it
parting the breakers with strokes
like a rapist pushing through
stormy wheat and he is safe and serious

on the sand like his hair
so night comes down upon
the familial anxieties of Vincent
he sleeps like a temple to no god

POEM

Hate is only one of many responses
true, hurt and hate go hand in hand
but why be afraid of hate, it is only there

think of filth, is it really awesome
neither is hate
don't be shy of unkindness, either
it's cleansing and allows you to be direct
like an arrow that feels something

out and out meanness, too, lets love breathe
you don't have to fight off getting in too deep
you can always get out if you're not too scared

an ounce of prevention's
enough to poison the heart
don't think of others
until you have thought of yourself, are true

all of these things, if you feel them
will be graced by a certain reluctance
and turn into gold

if felt by me, will be smilingly deflected
by your mysterious concern

POEM

I don't know as I get what D. H. Lawrence is driving at
when he writes of lust springing from the bowels
or do I
it could be the bowels of the earth
to lie flat on the earth in spring, summer or winter is sexy
you feel it stirring deep down slowly up to you
and sometimes it gives you a little nudge in the crotch
that's very sexy
and when someone looks sort of raggedy and dirty like Paulette Goddard
in *Modern Times* it's exciting, it isn't usual or attractive
perhaps D.H.L. is thinking of the darkness
certainly the crotch is light
and I suppose
any part of us that can only be seen by others
is a dark part
I feel that about the small of my back, too and the nape of my neck
they are dark
they are erotic zones as in the tropics
whereas Paris is straightforward and bright about it all
a coal miner has kind of a sexy occupation
though I'm sure it's painful down there

but so is lust
of light we can never have enough
but how would we find it
unless the darkness urged us on and into it
and I am dark
except when now and then it all comes clear
and I can see myself
as others luckily sometimes see me
in a good light

PERSONAL POEM

Now when I walk around at lunchtime
I have only two charms in my pocket
an old Roman coin Mike Kanemitsu gave me
and a bolt-head that broke off a packing case
when I was in Madrid the others never
brought me too much luck though they did
help keep me in New York against coercion
but now I'm happy for a time and interested

I walk through the luminous humidity
passing the House of Seagram with its wet
and its loungers and the construction to
the left that closed the sidewalk if
I ever get to be a construction worker
I'd like to have a silver hat please
and get to Moriarty's where I wait for
LeRoi and hear who wants to be a mover and
shaker the last five years my batting average

is .016 that's that, and LeRoi comes in
and tells me Miles Davis was clubbed 12
times last night outside BIRDLAND by a cop
a lady asks us for a nickel for a terrible
disease but we don't give her one we
don't like terrible diseases, then

we go eat some fish and some ale it's
cool but crowded we don't like Lionel Trilling
we decide, we like Don Allen we don't like
Henry James so much we like Herman Melville
we don't want to be in the poets' walk in
San Francisco even we just want to be rich
and walk on girders in our silver hats
I wonder if one person out of the 8,000,000 is
thinking of me as I shake hands with LeRoi
and buy a strap for my wristwatch and go
back to work happy at the thought possibly so

POST THE LAKE POETS BALLAD

Moving slowly sweating a lot
I am pushed by a gentle breeze
outside the Paradise Bar on
      St. Mark's Place and I breathe

and bourbon with Joe he says
did you see a letter from Larry
in the mailbox what a shame I didn't
      I wonder what it says

and then we eat and go to
The Horse Riders and my bum aches
from the hard seats and boredom
          is hard too we don't go

to the Cedar it's so hot out
and I read the letter which says
in your poems your gorgeous self-pity
          how do you like that

that is odd I think of myself
as a cheerful type who pretends to
be hurt to get a little depth into
          things that interest me

and I've even given that up
lately with the stream of events
going so fast and the movingly
          alternating with the amusingly

the depth all in the ocean
although I'm different in the winter
of course even this is a complaint
          but I'm happy anyhow

no more self-pity than Gertrude
Stein before Lucey Church or Savonarola
in the pulpit Allen Ginsberg at the
          Soviet Exposition am I Joe

NAPHTHA

Ah Jean Dubuffet
when you think of him
doing his military service in the Eiffel Tower
as a meteorologist
in 1922
you know how wonderful the 20th Century
can be
and the gaited Iroquois on the girders
fierce and unflinching-footed
nude as they should be
slightly empty
like a Sonia Delaunay
there is a parable of speed
somewhere behind the Indians' eyes
they invented the century with their horses
and their fragile backs
which are dark

we owe a debt to the Iroquois
and to Duke Ellington
for playing in the buildings when they are built
we don't do much ourselves
but fuck and think
of the haunting Métro
and the one who didn't show up there
while we were waiting to become part of our century
just as you can't make a hat out of steel
and still wear it
who wears hats anyway
it is our tribe's custom
to beguile

how are you feeling in ancient September
I am feeling like a truck on a wet highway

how can you
you were made in the image of god
I was not
I was made in the image of a sissy truck-driver
and Jean Dubuffet painting his cows
"with a likeness burst in the memory"
apart from love (don't say it)
I am ashamed of my century
for being so entertaining
but I have to smile

VARIATIONS ON PASTERNAK'S
"MEIN LIEBCHEN, WAS WILLST DU NOCH MEHR?"

Walls, except that they stretch through China
like a Way, are melancholy fingers in the snow
of years
          time moves, but is not moving in its strange grimace
the captive fights the distances within a flower of wire
and seldom wins a look from the dull tin receptacle he decorates

    not that anything is really there
the country is the city without houses, the city
merely a kissed country, a hamster of choices
whether you own forty cats or just three snakes you're rich
as you appear, miraculous appearance, I had forgotten
that things could be beautiful in the 20th Century under the moon

    the drabness of life peels away like an old recording by Lotte Lenya
it is not lucky to be German and you know it, though doom has held off

perhaps it is waiting like a smile in the sky
but no, it's the moon drifting and trudging
   and the clouds are imitating Diana Adams

               now the rain comes
and your face, like a child's soul, is parting its lids
   pouring down the brown plaster faces over doors and windows
over the casual elegancies of the last century and the poor
    over the lintels and the sniffs and the occasional hay fever
  to where nothing
             appears to be watering the city trees
            though they live, live on, as we do

what do you think has happened
that you have pushed the wall and
              stopped thinking of Bunny
  you have let death go, you have stopped
  you are not serene, you desire something, you are not ending
it is not that the world expects the people, but it does
the brassiness of weeds becomes sculptural and bridal
everything wants to be you and wisdom is unacceptable
  in the leaden world of fringes and distrust and duty

I have discovered that beneath the albatross there is a goose
  smiling
    a centenarian goes down the street and sees
   George Balanchine, that makes the day for him
just as the sight of you, no wall, no moon, no world, makes
              everything day to me

POEM

Khrushchev is coming on the right day!
                                        the cool graced light
is pushed off the enormous glass piers by hard wind
and everything is tossing, hurrying on up
                                        this country
has everything but *politesse,* a Puerto Rican cab driver says
and five different girls I see
                        look like Piedie Gimbel
with her blonde hair tossing too,
                                as she looked when I pushed
her little daughter on the swing on the lawn it was also windy

last night we went to a movie and came out,
                                        Ionesco is greater
than Beckett, Vincent said, that's what I think, blueberry blintzes
and Khrushchev was probably being carped at
                                        in Washington, no *politesse*
Vincent tells me about his mother's trip to Sweden
                                        Hans tells us
about his father's life in Sweden, it sounds like Grace Hartigan's
painting *Sweden*
                so I go home to bed and names drift through my head
Purgatorio Merchado, Gerhard Schwartz and Gaspar Gonzales, all
        unknown figures of the early morning as I go to work

where does the evil of the year go
                                when September takes New York
and turns it into ozone stalagmites
                                deposits of light
                                so I get back up
make coffee, and read François Villon, his life, so dark
    New York seems blinding and my tie is blowing up the street
I wish it would blow off
                        though it is cold and somewhat warms my neck

162

as the train bears Khrushchev on to Pennsylvania Station
     and the light seems to be eternal
     and joy seems to be inexorable
     I am foolish enough always to find it in wind

GETTING UP AHEAD OF SOMEONE (SUN)

I cough a lot (sinus?) so I
get up and have some tea with cognac
it is dawn
               the light flows evenly along the lawn
in chilly Southampton and I smoke
and hours and hours go by I read
van Vechten's *Spider Boy* then a short
story by Patsy Southgate and a poem
by myself it is cold and I shiver a little
in white shorts the day begun
so oddly not tired not nervous I
am for once truly awake letting it all
start slowly as I watch instead of
grabbing on late as usual
                         where did it go
                         it's not really awake yet
                         I will wait

and the house wakes up and goes
to get the dog in Sag Harbor I make
myself a bourbon and commence
to write one of my "I do this I do that"
poems in a sketch pad
                    it is tomorrow

though only six hours have gone by
each day's light has more significance these days

IN FAVOR OF ONE'S TIME

The spent purpose of a perfectly marvellous
life suddenly glimmers and leaps into flame
it's more difficult than you think to make charcoal
it's also pretty hard to remember life's marvellous
but there it is guttering choking then soaring
in the mirrored room of this consciousness
it's practically a blaze of pure sensibility
and however exaggerated at least something's going on
and the quick oxygen in the air will not go neglected
will not sulk or fall into blackness and peat

an angel flying slowly, curiously singes its wings
and you diminish for a moment out of respect
for beauty then flare up after all that's the angel
that wrestled with Jacob and loves conflict
as an athlete loves the tape, and we're off into
an immortal contest of actuality and pride
which is love assuming the consciousness of itself
as sky over all, medium of finding and founding
not just resemblance but the magnetic otherness
that that that stands erect in the spirit's glare
and waits for the joining of an opposite force's breath

so come the winds into our lives and last
longer than despair's sharp snake, crushed before it conquered

so marvellous is not just a poet's greenish namesake
and we live outside his garden in our tempestuous rights

LES LUTHS

Ah nuts! It's boring reading French newspapers
in New York as if I were a Colonial waiting for my gin
somewhere beyond this roof a jet is making a sketch of the sky
where is Gary Snyder I wonder if he's reading under a dwarf pine
stretched out so his book and his head fit under the lowest branch
while the sun of the Orient rolls calmly not getting through to him
not caring particularly because the light in Japan respects poets

while in Paris Monsieur Martory and his brother Jean the poet
are reading a piece by Matthieu Galey and preparing to send a *pneu*
everybody here is running around after dull pleasantries and
wondering if *The Hotel Wentley Poems* is as great as I say it is
and I am feeling particularly testy at being separated from
the one I love by the most dreary of practical exigencies money
when I want only to lean on my elbow and stare into space feeling
the one warm beautiful thing in the world breathing upon my right rib

what are lutes they make ugly twangs and rest on knees in cafés
I want to hear only your light voice running on about Florida
as we pass the changing traffic light and buy grapes for wherever
we will end up praising the mattressless sleigh-bed and the
Mexican egg and the clock that will not make me know
        how to leave you

POEM

Now it is the 27th
of this month
which would have been my birthday
if I'd been born in it
but I wasn't
would have made me a
Scorpion
which symbolizes silver, money, riches
firm in aim, coldblooded in action
loving the Bull
smelling of sandalwood
I do anyway

instead of
Cancer
which symbolizes instability, suggestibility, sensibility
all the ilities like a clavichord
only an interior firmness
favoring good and evil alike
loving Capricorn
with its solitudinous research

but how could I love other
than the worldly Virgin
my force is in mobility it's said
I move
towards you
born in the sign which I should only like
with love

POEM

To Donald M. Allen

Now the violets are all gone, the rhinoceroses, the cymbals
a grisly pale has settled over the stockyard where the fur flies
and the sound
                         is that of a bulldozer in heat stuck in the mud
where a lilac still scrawnily blooms and cries out "Walt!"
so they repair the street in the middle of the night
and Allen and Peter can once again walk forth to visit friends
in the illuminated moonlight over the mists and the towers
having mistakenly thought that Bebe Daniels was in *I Cover the Waterfront*
instead of Claudette Colbert it has begun to rain softly and I walk
slowly thinking of becoming a stalk of asparagus for Hallowe'en
        which idea Vincent poopoos as not being really 40s
so the weight
                         of the rain drifting amiably is like a sentimental breeze
and seems to have been invented by a collapsed Kim Novak balloon

yet Janice is helping Kenneth appeal to The Ford Foundation in
her manner oft described as The Sweet Succinct and Ned is glad
        not to be up too late
                                            for the sake of his music and his ear
            where discipline finds itself singing and even screaming away

I shall not dine another night like this with Robin and Don and Joe
as lightly as the day is gone but that was earlier
                                                            a knock on the door
my heart your heart

            my head and the strange reality of our flesh in the rain
so many parts of a strange existence independent but not searching in the night
                    nor in the morning when the rain has stopped

POEM V (F) W

I don't know if you doubt it
but I think you do
I am independent of the Cabaret Voltaire
the Café Grinzing the Black Cat
the anubis
two parallel lines always meet
except mentally
which brings on their quarrels
and if I sit down I admit
it is not at a table
underneath elms
to read

you were walking down a street softened by rain
and your footsteps were quiet
and I came around the corner
inside the room
to close the window
and thought what a beautiful person
and it was you
no I was coming out the door
and you looked sad
which you later said was tired
and I was glad
you had wanted to see me
and we went forward
back to my room
to be alone in your mysterious look

among the relics of postwar hysterical pleasures
I see my vices
lying like abandoned works of art
which I created so eagerly
to be worldly and modern

and with it
what I can't remember
I see them with your eyes

POEM

"À la recherche de Gertrude Stein"

When I am feeling depressed and anxious sullen
all you have to do is take your clothes off
and all is wiped away revealing life's tenderness
that we are flesh and breathe and are near us
as you are really as you are I become as I
really am alive and knowing vaguely what is
and what is important to me above the intrusions
of incident and accidental relationships
which have nothing to do with my life

when I am in your presence I feel life is strong
and will defeat all its enemies and all of mine
and all of yours and yours in you and mine in me
sick logic and feeble reasoning are cured
by the perfect symmetry of your arms and legs
spread out making an eternal circle together
creating a golden pillar beside the Atlantic
the faint line of hair dividing your torso
gives my mind rest and emotions their release
into the infinite air where since once we are
together we always will be in this life come what may

POEM

Light   clarity   avocado salad in the morning
after all the terrible things I do how amazing it is
to find forgiveness and love, not even forgiveness
since what is done is done and forgiveness isn't love
and love is love nothing can ever go wrong
though things can get irritating boring and dispensable
(in the imagination) but not really for love
though a block away you feel distant the mere presence
changes everything like a chemical dropped on a paper
and all thoughts disappear in a strange quiet excitement
I am sure of nothing but this, intensified by breathing

HÔTEL TRANSYLVANIE

Shall we win at love or shall we lose
                              can it be
that hurting and being hurt is a trick forcing the love
we want to appear, that the hurt is a card
and is it black? is it red? is it a paper, dry of tears
chevalier, change your expression! the wind is sweeping over
the gaming tables ruffling the cards/they are black and red
like a Futurist torture and how do you know it isn't always there
waiting while doubt is the father that has you kidnapped by friends

      yet you will always live in a jealous society of accident
you will never know how beautiful you are or how beautiful
the other is, you will continue to refuse to die for yourself

you will continue to sing on trying to cheer everyone up
and they will know as they listen with excessive pleasure that you're dead
        and they will not mind that they have let you entertain
at the expense of the only thing you want in the world/you are amusing
as a game is amusing when someone is forced to lose as in a game ᵀ must

            oh *hôtel,* you should be merely a bed
surrounded by walls where two souls meet and do nothing but breathe
breathe in breathe out fuse illuminate confuse *stick* dissemble
but not as cheaters at cards have something to win/you have only to be
as you are being, as you must be, as you always are, as you shall be forever
no matter what fate deals you or the imagination discards like a tyrant
as the drums descend and summon the hatchet over the tinselled realities

you know that I am not here to fool around, that I must win or die
I expect you to do everything because it is of no consequence/no duel
you must rig the deck you must make me win at whatever cost to the reputation
of the establishment/sublime moment of dishonest hope/I must win
for if the floods of tears arrive they will wash it all away
                                    and then
you will know what it is to want something, but you may not be allowed
to die as I have died, you may only be allowed to drift downstream
to another body of inimical attractions for which you will substitute/distrust
and I will have had my revenge on the black bitch of my nature which you
                    love as I have never loved myself

but I hold on/I am lyrical to a fault/I do not despair being too foolish
where will you find me, projective verse, since I will be gone?
for six seconds of your beautiful face I will sell the hotel and commit
an uninteresting suicide in Louisiana where it will take them a long time
to know who I am/why I came there/what and why I am and made to happen

POEM

So many echoes in my head
that when I am frantic to do something
about anything, out comes "you were wearing . . ."
or I knock my head against a wall
of my own appetite for despair and come
up with "you once ran naked toward me/Knee
deep in cold March surf" or I blame it
on Blake, on Robert Aldrich's *Kiss Me,
Deadly,* on the "latitude" of the stars

but where in all this noise
am I waiting for the clouds to be blown
away away away away away into the sun
(burp), I wouldn't want the clouds to be
burped back by that hot optimistic cliché, it
hangs always promising some nebulous
healthy reaction to our native dark

I will let the sun wait till summer
now that our love has moved into the dark
area symbolizing depth and secrecy and mystery
it's not bad, we shall find out
when the light returns what the new
season means/when others' interpretations
have gotten back up onto the pedestals
we gave them
                    so long as we are still
wearing each other when alone

POEM

That's not a cross look it's a sign of life
but I'm glad you care how I look at you
this morning (after I got up) I was thinking
of President Warren G. Harding and Horace S.
Warren, father of the little blonde girl
across the street and another blonde Agnes
Hedlund (this was in the 6th grade!)   what

now the day has begun in a soft grey way
with elephantine traffic trudging along Fifth
and two packages of Camels in my pocket
I can't think of one interesting thing Warren
G. Harding did, I guess I was passing notes
to Sally and Agnes at the time he came up
in our elephantine history course everything

seems slow suddenly and boring except
for my insatiable thinking towards you
as you lie asleep completely plotzed and
gracious as a hillock in the mist from one
small window, sunless and only slightly open
as is your mouth and presently your quiet eyes
your breathing is like that history lesson

AVENUE A

We hardly ever see the moon any more
                                    so no wonder
        it's so beautiful when we look up suddenly
and there it is gliding broken-faced over the bridges
brilliantly coursing, soft, and a cool wind fans
            your hair over your forehead and your memories
                of Red Grooms' locomotive landscape
I want some bourbon/you want some oranges/I love the leather
                jacket Norman gave me
                                    and the corduroy coat David
        gave you, it is more mysterious than spring, the El Greco
heavens breaking open and then reassembling like lions
                                    in a vast tragic veldt
        that is far from our small selves and our temporally united
passions in the cathedral of Januaries

        everything is too comprehensible
these are my delicate and caressing poems
I suppose there will be more of those others to come, as in the past
                                    so many!
but for now the moon is revealing itself like a pearl
                                    to my equally naked heart

NOW THAT I AM IN MADRID AND CAN THINK

I think of you
and the continents brilliant and arid
and the slender heart you are sharing my share of with the American air

as the lungs I have felt sonorously subside slowly greet each morning
and your brown lashes flutter revealing two perfect dawns colored by New York

see a vast bridge stretching to the humbled outskirts with only you
                standing on the edge of the purple like an only tree

and in Toledo the olive groves' soft blue look at the hills with silver
                like glasses like an old lady's hair
it's well known that God and I don't get along together
it's just a view of the brass works to me, I don't care about the Moors
seen through you the great works of death, you are greater

you are smiling, you are emptying the world so we can be alone

HAVING A COKE WITH YOU

is even more fun than going to San Sebastian, Irún, Hendaye, Biarritz, Bayonne
or being sick to my stomach on the Travesera de Gracia in Barcelona
partly because in your orange shirt you look like a better happier St. Sebastian
partly because of my love for you, partly because of your love for yoghurt
partly because of the fluorescent orange tulips around the birches
partly because of the secrecy our smiles take on before people and statuary
it is hard to believe when I'm with you that there can be anything as still
as solemn as unpleasantly definitive as statuary when right in front of it
in the warm New York 4 o'clock light we are drifting back and forth
between each other like a tree breathing through its spectacles

and the portrait show seems to have no faces in it at all, just paint
you suddenly wonder why in the world anyone ever did them
                                                I look
at you and I would rather look at you than all the portraits in the world

except possibly for the *Polish Rider* occasionally and anyway it's in the Frick
which thank heavens you haven't gone to yet so we can go together the first time
and the fact that you move so beautifully more or less takes care of Futurism
just as at home I never think of the *Nude Descending a Staircase* or
at a rehearsal a single drawing of Leonardo or Michelangelo that used to wow me
and what good does all the research of the Impressionists do them
when they never got the right person to stand near the tree when the sun sank
or for that matter Marino Marini when he didn't pick the rider as carefully
as the horse
                    it seems they were all cheated of some marvellous experience
which is not going to go wasted on me which is why I'm telling you about it

ODE TO TANAQUIL LECLERCQ

Smiling through my own memories of painful excitement your wide eyes
stare
          and narrow like a lost forest of childhood stolen from gypsies
two eyes that are the sunset of
                              two knees
                                    two wrists
                                          two minds
and the extended philosophical column, when they conducted the dialogues
              in distant Athens, rests on your two ribbon-wrapped hearts, white
          credibly agile
                    flashing
                         scimitars of a city-state

where in the innocence of my watching had those ribbons become entangled
              dragging me upward into lilac-colored ozone where I gasped
                    and you continued to smile as you dropped the bloody scarf of my life
                              from way up there, my neck hurt

you were always changing into something else
and always will be
always plumage, perfection's broken heart, wings

and wide eyes in which everything you do
repeats yourself simultaneously and simply
                    as a window "gives" on something

it seems sometimes as if you were only breathing
        and everything happened around you
because when you disappeared in the wings nothing was there
        but the motion of some extraordinary happening I hadn't understood
the superb arc of a question, of a decision about death

        because you are beautiful you are hunted
            and with the courage of a vase
                    you refuse to become a deer or tree
            and the world holds its breath
                    to see if you are there, and safe

                        are you?

POEM

O sole mio, hot diggety, nix "I wather think I can"
come to see *Go into Your Dance* on TV—*HELEN MORGAN!? GLENDA FARRELL!?*
1935!?
        it reminds me of my first haircut, or an elm tree or something!
or did I fall off my bicycle when my grandmother came back from Florida?

        you see I have always wanted things to be beautiful
        and now, for a change, they are!

STEPS

How funny you are today New York
like Ginger Rogers in *Swingtime*
and St. Bridget's steeple leaning a little to the left

here I have just jumped out of a bed full of V-days
(I got tired of D-days) and blue you there still
accepts me foolish and free
all I want is a room up there
and you in it
and even the traffic halt so thick is a way
for people to rub up against each other
and when their surgical appliances lock
they stay together
for the rest of the day (what a day)
I go by to check a slide and I say
that painting's not so blue

where's Lana Turner
she's out eating
and Garbo's backstage at the Met
everyone's taking their coat off
so they can show a rib-cage to the rib-watchers
and the park's full of dancers with their tights and shoes
in little bags
who are often mistaken for worker-outers at the West Side Y
why not
the Pittsburgh Pirates shout because they won
and in a sense we're all winning
we're alive

the apartment was vacated by a gay couple
who moved to the country for fun
they moved a day too soon
even the stabbings are helping the population explosion

though in the wrong country
and all those liars have left the U N
the Seagram Building's no longer rivalled in interest
not that we need liquor (we just like it)

and the little box is out on the sidewalk
next to the delicatessen
so the old man can sit on it and drink beer
and get knocked off it by his wife later in the day
while the sun is still shining

oh god it's wonderful
to get out of bed
and drink too much coffee
and smoke too many cigarettes
and love you so much

AVE MARIA

Mothers of America
                    let your kids go to the movies!
get them out of the house so they won't know what you're up to
it's true that fresh air is good for the body
                                        but what about the soul
that grows in darkness, embossed by silvery images
and when you grow old as grow old you must
                                        they won't hate you
they won't criticize you they won't know
                                they'll be in some glamorous country
they first saw on a Saturday afternoon or playing hookey

they may even be grateful to you
                                    for their first sexual experience
which only cost you a quarter
                                    and didn't upset the peaceful home
they will know where candy bars come from
                                                and gratuitous bags of popcorn
as gratuitous as leaving the movie before it's over
with a pleasant stranger whose apartment is in the Heaven on Earth Bldg
near the Williamsburg Bridge
                                    oh mothers you will have made the little tykes
so happy because if nobody does pick them up in the movies
they won't know the difference
                                    and if somebody does it'll be sheer gravy
and they'll have been truly entertained either way
instead of hanging around the yard
                                    or up in their room
                                                        hating you
prematurely since you won't have done anything horribly mean yet
except keeping them from the darker joys
                                            it's unforgivable the latter
so don't blame me if you won't take this advice
                                            and the family breaks up
and your children grow old and blind in front of a TV set
                                                        seeing
movies you wouldn't let them see when they were young

WHAT APPEARS TO BE YOURS

The root   an acceptable connection
ochre   except meaning–dream partly
where the will falters   a screw polished

180

a whole pair of shutters   you saw it
I went in the door   the umbrella
apart from the hole you see a slide   up
two blue   yes the wind mutters
it slides and gulps   it is the snow
where   your breast pocket   exception
to the rule   whenever the beast moves
a lion   is the same at lunch as at dinner
tow-head   your heaviness is rather exciting
ai-ai   driving the taxi into the ai
where to   whereto   yet an appendix
stops the trip   on the East River Drive
zooming downtown to Jap's   eating
later a bevy of invitations   a Chinese bar
what done   undone   a long wait for rain
you were under the settee   eating cough drops
I mean nougatines   where are you now
whose hand   behind the pale Housatonic   I
waited   wait   will wait
and what fun it is   Great Northern Hotel
and the sole of a foot   substantial in the snow
warm   through a hole in the stocking   the sky

CORNKIND

So the rain falls
it drops all over the place
and where it finds a little rock pool
it fills it up with dirt
and the corn grows
a green Bette Davis sits under it

reading a volume of William Morris
oh fertility! beloved of the Western world
you aren't so popular in China
though they fuck too

and do I really want a son
to carry on my idiocy past the Horned Gates
poor kid   a staggering load

yet it can happen casually
and he lifts a little of the load each day
as I become more and more idiotic
and grows to be a strong strong man
and one day carries as I die
my final idiocy and the very gates
into a future of his choice

but what of William Morris
what of you Million Worries
what of Bette Davis in
AN EVENING WITH WILLIAM MORRIS
or THE WORLD OF SAMUEL GREENBERG

what of Hart Crane
what of phonograph records and gin

what of "what of"

you are of me, that's what
and that's the meaning of fertility
hard and moist and moaning

FOR THE CHINESE NEW YEAR
& FOR BILL BERKSON

One or another
Is lost, since we fall apart
Endlessly, in one motion depart
From each other.—D. H. Lawrence

Behind New York there's a face
and it's not Sibelius's with a cigar
it was red it was strange and hateful
and then I became a child again
like a nadir or a zenith or a nudnik

what do you think this is my youth
and the aged future that is sweeping me away
carless and gasless under the Sutton
and Beekman Places towards a hellish rage
it is there that face I fear under ramps

it is perhaps the period that ends
the problem as a proposition of days of days
just an attack on the feelings that stay
poised in the hurricane's center that
eye through which only camels can pass

but I do not mean that tenderness doesn't
linger like a Paris afternoon or a wart
something dumb and despicable that I love
because it is silent oh what difference
does it make me into some kind of space statistic

a lot is buried under that smile
a lot of sophistication gone down the drain
to become the mesh of a mythical fish
at which we never stare back never stare back
where there is so much downright forgery

under that I find it restful like a bush
some people are outraged by cleanliness

I hate the lack of smells myself and yet I stay
it is better than being actually present
and the stare can swim away into the past

can adorn it with easy convictions rat
cow tiger rabbit dragon snake horse sheep
monkey rooster dog and pig "Flower Drum Song"
so that nothing is vain not the gelded sand
not the old spangled lotus not my fly

which I have thought about but never really
looked at well that's a certain orderliness
of personality "if you're brought up Protestant
enough a Catholic" oh shit on the beaches so
what if I did look up your trunks and see it

II
then the parallel becomes an eagle parade
of Busby Berkeleyites marching marching half-toe
I suppose it's the happiest moment in infinity
because we're dissipated and tired and fond no
I don't think psychoanalysis shrinks the spleen

here we are and what the hell are we going to do
with it we are going to blow it up like daddy did
only us I really think we should go up for a change
I'm tired of always going down what price glory
it's one of those timeless priceless words like come
well now how does your conscience feel about that
would you rather explore tomorrow with a sponge
there's no need to look for a target you're it
like in childhood when the going was aimed at a
sandwich it all depends on which three of us are there

but here come the prophets with their loosening nails
it is only as blue as the lighting under the piles
I have something portentous to say to you but which

of the papier-mâché languages do you understand you
don't dare to take it off paper much less put it on

yes it is strange that everyone fucks and every-
one mentions it and it's boring too that faded floor
how many teeth have chewed a little piece of the lover's
flesh how many teeth are there in the world it's like
Harpo Marx smiling at a million pianos call that Africa

call it New Guinea call it Poughkeepsie I guess
it's love I guess the season of renunciation is at "hand"
the final fatal hour of turpitude and logic demise
is when you miss getting rid of something delouse
is when you don't louse something up which way is the inn

III
I'm looking for a million-dollar heart in a carton
of frozen strawberries like the Swedes where is sunny England
and those fields where they stillbirth the wars why
did they suddenly stop playing why is Venice a Summer
Festival and not New York were you born in America

the inscrutable passage of a lawn mower punctuates
the newly installed Muzack in the Shubert Theatre am I nuts
or is this the happiest moment of my life who's arguing it's
I mean 'tis lawd sakes it took daddy a long time to have
that accident so Ant Grace could get completely into black

didn't you know we was all going to be Zen Buddhists after
what we did you sure don't know much about war-guilt
or nothin and the peach trees continued to rejoice around
the prick which was for once authorized by our Congress
though inactive what if it had turned out to be a volcano

that's a mulatto of another nationality of marble
it's time for dessert I don't care what street this is
you're not telling me to take a tour are you
I don't want to look at any fingernails or any toes
I just want to go on being subtle and dead like life

I'm not naturally so detached but I think
they might send me up any minute so I try to be free
you know we've all sinned a lot against science
so we really ought to be available as an apple on a bough
pleasant thought fresh air free love cross-pollenization

oh oh god how I'd love to dream let alone sleep it's night
the soft air wraps me like a swarm it's raining and I have
a cold I am a real human being with real ascendancies
and a certain amount of rapture what do you do with a kid
like me if you don't eat me I'll have to eat myself

it's a strange curse my "generation" has we're all
like the flowers in the Agassiz Museum perpetually ardent
don't touch me because when I tremble it makes a noise
like a Chinese wind-bell it's that I'm seismographic is all
and when a Jesuit has stared you down for ever after you clink

I wonder if I've really scrutinized this experience like
you're supposed to have if you can type there's not much
soup left on my sleeve energy creativity guts ponderableness
lent is coming in imponderableness "I'd like to die smiling" ugh
and a very small tiptoe is crossing the threshold away

whither Lumumba whither oh whither Gauguin
I have often tried to say goodbye to strange fantoms I
read about in the newspapers and have always succeeded
though the ones at "home" are dependent on Dependable
Laboratory and Sales Company on Pulaski Street strange

I think it's goodbye to a lot of things like Christmas
and the Mediterranean and halos and meteorites and villages
full of damned children well it's goodbye then as in Strauss
or some other desperately theatrical venture it's goodbye
to lunch to love to evil things and to the ultimate good as "well"

the strange career of a personality begins at five and ends
forty minutes later in a fog the rest is just a lot of stranded

ships honking their horns full of joy-seeking cadets in bloomers
and beards it's okay with me but must they cheer while they honk
it seems that breath could easily fill a balloon and drift away

scaring the locusts in the straggling grey of living dumb
exertions then the useful noise would come of doom of data
turned to elegant decoration like a strangling prince once ordered
no there is no precedent of history no history nobody came before
nobody will ever come before and nobody ever was that man

you will not die not knowing this is true this year

ESSAY ON STYLE

Someone else's Leica sitting on the table
the black kitchen table I am painting
the floor yellow, Bill is painting it
wouldn't you know my mother would call
up
   and complain?
                    my sister's pregnant and
went to the country for the weekend without
telling her
          in point of fact why don't I
go out to have dinner with her or "let her"
come in? well if Mayor Wagner won't allow private
cars on Manhattan because of the snow, I
will probably never see her again
                        considering
my growingly more perpetual state and how

can one say that angel in the Frick's wings
are "attached" if it's a real angel? now

I was reflecting the other night meaning
I was being reflected upon that Sheridan Square
is remarkably beautiful, sitting in JACK
DELANEY's looking out the big race-track window
on the wet
                    drinking a cognac while Edwin
read my new poem it occurred to me how impossible
it is to fool Edwin not that I don't know as
much as the next about obscurity in modern verse
but he
            always knows what it's about as well
as what it is do you think we can ever
strike *as* and *but,* too, out of the language
then we can attack *well* since it has no
application whatsoever neither as a state
of being or a rest for the mind no such
things available
                        where do you think I've
got to? the spectacle of a grown man
decorating
                a Christmas tree disgusts me that's
where
            that's one of the places yetbutaswell
I'm glad I went to that party for Ed Dorn
last night though he didn't show up do you think
,Bill, we can get rid of *though* also, and *also*?
maybe your
                lettrism is the only answer treating
the typewriter as an intimate organ why not?
nothing else is (intimate)
                                no I am not going
to have you "in" for dinner nor am I going "out"
I am going to eat alone for the rest of my life

MARY DESTI'S ASS

In Bayreuth once
we were very good friends of the Wagners
and I stepped in once
for Isadora so perfectly
she would never allow me to dance again
that's the way it was in Bayreuth

the way it was in Hackensack
was different
there one never did anything
and everyone hated you anyway
it was fun, it was clear
you knew where you stood

in Boston you were never really standing
I was usually lying
it was amusing to be lying all
the time for everybody
it was like exercise

it means something to exercise
in Norfolk Virginia
it means you've been to bed with a Nigra
well it is exercise
the only difference is it's better than Boston

I was walking along the street
of Cincinnati
and I met Kenneth Koch's mother
fresh from the Istanbul Hilton
she liked me and I liked her
we both liked Istanbul

then in Waukegan I met a furniture manufacturer
and it wiped out all dreams of pleasantness from my mind

it was like being pushed down hard
on a chair
it was like something horrible you hadn't expected
which is the most horrible thing

and in Singapore I got a dreadful
disease it was amusing to have bumps
except they went into my veins
and rose to the surface like Vesuvius
getting cured was like learning to smoke

yet I always loved Baltimore
the porches which hurt your ass
no, they were the steps
well you have a wet ass anyway
if they'd only stop scrubbing

and Frisco where I saw
Toumanova "the baby ballerina" except
she looked like a cow
I didn't know the history of the ballet yet
not that that taught me much

now if you feel like you want to deal with
Tokyo
you've really got something to handle
it's like Times Square at midnight
you don't know where you're going
but you know

and then in Harbin I knew
how to behave it was glorious that
was love sneaking up on me through the snow
and I felt it was because of all
the postcards and the smiles and kisses and the grunts
that was love but I kept on traveling

POEM

Twin spheres full of fur and noise
rolling softly up my belly beddening on my chest
and then my mouth is full of suns
that softness seems so anterior to that hardness
that mouth that is used to talking too much
speaks at last of the tenderness of Ancient China
and the love of form the Odyssies
each tendril is covered with seed pearls
your hair is like a tree in an ice storm
jetting I commit the immortal spark jetting
you give that form to my life the Ancients loved
those suns are smiling as they move across the sky
and as your chariot I soon become a myth
which heaven is it that we inhabit for so long a time
it must be discovered soon and disappear

ST. PAUL AND ALL THAT

Totally abashed and smiling

                                 I walk in
                                 sit down and
                                 face the frigidaire

               it's April
               no May
               it's May

such little things have to be established in morning

after the big things of night
                    do you want me to come? when
I think of all the things I've been thinking of I feel insane
simply "life in Birmingham is hell"
                              simply "you will miss me
                                   but that's good"
when the tears of a whole generation are assembled
they will only fill a coffee cup
                              just because they evaporate
doesn't mean life has heat
                         "this various dream of living"
I am alive with you
              full of anxious pleasures and pleasurable anxiety
hardness and softness
                   listening while you talk and talking while you read
I read what you read
              you do not read what I read
which is right, I am the one with the curiosity
         you read for some mysterious reason
                              I read simply because I am a writer
the sun doesn't necessarily set, sometimes it just disappears
         when you're not here someone walks in and says
                                             "hey,
there's no dancer in that bed"
                         O the Polish summers! those drafts!
                         those black and white teeth!
you never come when you say you'll come but on the other hand you do come

SUMMER BREEZES

(*F.Y.(M.)M.B.I.*)

An element of mischief contributed
                                    to the float
                                    in the lake
                    the pool stood on its ear, dripping aqua
                                                irritating eyes
they swam all day in the torrid cool
                    and at night they sunned each other
it was idyllic
                    there was a lot of space between them
                                                it was not a grave
then Uncle Ned came and ruined everything
Lois said she was pregnant
the gardener said he was guilty
Lois said he wasn't
                    what an eruption!
                                    (everyone knew it was Cherry
                                    he played basketball winters)
            mother flew in from Des Moines
                                        with her dog
the whole damn vacation was really ruined!
                                        it wasn't so much
what happened as having all those people around, I thought

            yet when Lois got fired I was sorry
            I was very fond of Cherry

            (AND OTHER BREEZES)
which made me think a lot
                    (that *Gone With the Wind* must be right) and
I looked and looked, but there was nobody for me to do anything with
what a summer!
            so I lay on the float on my belly and thought of
Indians (Eastern and Western, but mostly Western—Apache and Iroquois,
that is)

Zanzibar   shishkebab   South Seas   sharks
ridingboots   lotusleaves   whippings   lipstick   unicorns
    panthers (preferably black panthers, no, preferably blonde panthers)
tigersandleopardstoo   champagneandothermoviedrinks   blood
pearls   snow   windycrevasses   a gigantic tornado followed
immediately by the eruption of the biggest volcano in the world and
the crash of an oversized comet!

> and that summer my swimming improved
>
> a lot

F. (MISSIVE & WALK) I. #53

I'm getting tired of not wearing underwear
and then again I like it
                 strolling along
feeling the wind blow softly on my genitals
though I also like them encased in something
firm, almost tight, like a projectile
                          at
a streetcorner I stop and a lamppost is
bending over the traffic pensively like a
praying mantis, not lighting anything,
just looking
            who dropped that empty carton
of cracker jacks I wonder I find the favor
that's a good sign
            it's the blue everyone
is talking about an enormous cloud which hides
the observatory blimp   when you
ride on a 5th Avenue bus you hide on a 5th

Avenue bus I mean compared to you walking
don't hide   there you are trying
to hide behind a fire hydrant   I'm
not going to the Colisseum I'm going to
the Russian Tea Room fooled you didn't I
well   it is nicer in the Park
with the pond and all that   okay
lake   and bicyclists give you
a feeling of being at leisure in the open
air lazy and good-tempered   which is
fairly unusual these days   I liked
for instance   carrying my old Gautier book
and *L'Ombra* over to LeRoi's the other
pale afternoon through the crowds of 3rd
Avenue and the ambulance and the drunk

PETIT POÈME EN PROSE

Connais-tu peut-être la chanson ancienne "C'était un étranger"
in troubadour times it was very popular and made people act promiscuous
even though there were no subways then
elle continuait, cette chanson
"tu as tué mon coeur, 'tit voyou"
which is strange when you think of it
I don't believe the Church would have sanctioned that sort of thing
and besides it was sung to the air which later became
"Connais-tu le pays
où le citron fleurit"
an unimaginable sentiment
for Mignon! a voyou yet!

cherishing these reflections as I walked along, I came to a garbage dump
the poured concrete dome of which
was covered with children's inscriptions
the most interesting of which
was "I ate you up"
it was not a very interesting dump
so I pursued my "course" of thought
"tu es mon amour depuis . . ." oh no, not
that, and then "Ich fühle ein kleiner . . ."
unh unh
yet simply to walk, walk on, did not seem nearly enough for my rabid nerves
so I began to hum the Beer Barrel Polka
hopping and skipping along
in my scarf which came to my heels
and soon caught on a door knob

I was back in town!
what a relief!
I popped into the nearest movie-house and saw two marvelous Westerns
but, alas! this is all I remember of the magnificent poem I made on my walk
why are you reading this poem anyway?

MOZART CHEMISIER

For instance you walk in and faint
you are being one with Africa
I saw the soda standing next to the bay stallion
it was still foaming it had what is called a head on it
then I went and had a double carbonated bourbon on the porch
in the moonlight the poplars looked like aspidistra
over the unexperienced lake
wait, wait a while it all kept murmuring

but I know that always makes me so sad
there was a lot of tinselly sky out which irritated me too
and my anger is strictly European plan plan
now why would I get up and dance around
you see it is all very beautiful
the emphasis being on suds, suds in the lake, suds in my heart
luckily when the lake the tree was tempting me
I didn't have any white toreador pants
back at the ranch they were serving bubbly gin so I ran down the trail
so short a trail
so sweet a smell hay in your ears it's hot
oh world why are you so easy to figure out
beneath the ground there is something beautiful
I've had enough of sky
it's so obvious
everyone thinks they're going up
in these here America
put on your earrings we're going to the railroad station
I don't care how small the house they live in is
you don't have any earrings
I don't have a ticket

FIRST DANCES

I
From behind he takes her waist
and lifts her, her lavender waist
stained with tears and her mascara
is running, her neck is tired
from drooping. She floats she steps
automatically correct, then suddenly
she is alive up there and smiles.

How much greater triumph for him
that she had so despaired when his
hands encircled her like a pillar
and lifted her into the air
which after him will turn to rock-
like boredom, but not till after
many hims and he will not be there.

2

The punch bowl was near the cloakroom
so the pints could be taken out of the
boys' cloaks and dumped into the punch.
Outside the branches beat hysterically
towards the chandeliers, just fended
off by fearful windows. The chandeliers
giggle a little. There were many
introductions but few invitations. I
found a spot of paint on my coat as
others found pimples. It is easy to
dance it is even easy to dance together
sometimes. We were very young and ugly
we knew it, everybody knew it.

3

A white hall inside a church. Nerves.

ANSWER TO VOZNESENSKY & EVTUSHENKO

We are tired of your tiresome imitations of Mayakovsky
we are tired
            of your dreary tourist ideas of our Negro selves
our selves are in far worse condition than the obviousness

of your color sense
                        your general sense of Poughkeepsie is
a gaucherie no American poet would be guilty of in Tiflis
thanks to French Impressionism
                                    we do not pretend to know more
than can be known
                        how many sheets have you stained with your semen
oh Tartars, and how many
                            of our loves have you illuminated with
your heart your breath
                            as we poets of America have loved you
your countrymen, our countrymen, our lives, your lives, and
the dreary expanses of your translations
                                        your idiotic manifestos
and the strange black cock which has become ours despite your envy

we do what we feel
                        you do not even do what you must or can
I do not love you any more since Mayakovsky died and Pasternak
theirs was the death of my nostalgia for your tired ignorant race
since you insist on race
                            you shall not take my friends away from me
because they live in Harlem
                                you shall not make Mississippi into Sakhalin
you came too late, a lovely talent doesn't make a ball
    I consider myself to be black and you not even part
where you see death
                        you see a dance of death
                                                which is
imperialist, implies training, requires techniques
our ballet does not employ
                            you are indeed as cold as wax
as your progenitor was red, and how greatly we loved his redness
in the fullness of our own idiotic sun! what
"roaring universe" outshouts his violent triumphant sun!
        you are not even speaking
                                in a whisper
    Mayakovsky's hat worn by a horse

FANTASY

(dedicated to the health of Allen Ginsberg)

How do you like the music of Adolph

Deutsch? I like

it, I like it better than Max Steiner's. Take his

score for *Northern Pursuit,* the Helmut Dantine theme

was . . .

and then the window fell on my hand. Errol

Flynn was skiing by. Down

down down went the grim

grey submarine under the "cold" ice.

Helmut was

safely ashore, on the ice.

What dreams, what incredible

fantasies of snow farts will this all lead to?

I

don't know, I have stopped thinking like a sled dog.

The main thing is to tell a story.

It is almost

very important. Imagine

throwing away the avalanche

so early in the movie. I am the only spy left

in Canada,

but just because I'm alone in the snow

doesn't necessarily mean I'm a Nazi.

Let's see,

two aspirins a vitamin C tablet and some baking soda

should do the trick, that's practically an

Alka

Seltzer. Allen come out of the bathroom

and take it.

I think someone put butter on my skis instead

of wax.

Ouch. The leanto is falling over in the

firs, and there is another fatter spy here. They

didn't tell me they sent
                        him. Well, that takes care
of him, boy were those huskies hungry.
                                    Allen,
are you feeling any better? Yes, I'm crazy about
Helmut Dantine
                    but I'm glad that Canada will remain
free. Just free, that's all, never argue with the movies.

BIOTHERM (FOR BILL BERKSON)

The best thing in the world   but I better be quick about it
better be gone tomorrow
                                better be gone last night and
                next Thursday better be gone
better be
                        always   or what's the use the sky
        the endless clouds trailing we leading them by the bandanna, red

you meet the Ambassador   "a year and a half of trying to make him"
        he is dressed in red, he has a red ribbon down his chest he
        has   7   gold decorations pinned to his gash
he sleeps a lot, thinks a lot, fucks a lot, impenetrable and Jude-ish
        I love him, you would love him too   if you could see outside

                        whoops-musicale (sei tu m'ami) ahhahahahaha
                        loppy di looploop   which is why   I suppose
        Leontyne Price asked Secretary Goldberg to intervene with Metropera
it's not as dangerous as you think
                                NEVERTHELESS (thank you, Aristotle)

      I know you are interested in the incongruities of my behavior, John
just as Bill you are interested in the blue paint JA Oscar Maxine Khnute
perhaps you'd better be particularly interested   POOF

                                  extended vibrations
ziggurats ZIG I to IV   stars of the Tigris-Euphrates basin
    leading ultimates such as kickapoo joyjuice halvah Canton cheese
in thimbles
                    paraded for gain, but yet a parade kiss me,
                            Busby Berkeley, kiss me
you have ended the war by simply singing in your Irene Dunne foreskin
"Practically Yours"
                with June Vincent, Lionello Venturi and Casper Citron
        a Universal-International release produced by G. Mennen Williams
                      directed by Florine Stettheimer
                      continuity by the Third Reich
     after "hitting" the beach at Endzoay we drank up the liebfraumilch
            and pushed on up the Plata to the pampas
       you didn't pick up the emeralds you god-damned fool you got
            no collarbone you got no dish no ears
                      Maurice Prendergast
                      Tilly Losch
               "when the seizure tuck 'im 'e went" — Colette
besides, the snow was snowing, our fault for calling the ticket
                  perhaps at the end of a very strange game
          you won   ? (?) ! (?)
    and that is important (yeah) to win (yeah)

bent on his knees the Old Mariner said where the fuck
    is that motel you told me about mister I aint come here for no clams
I want swimmingpool mudpacks the works carbonateddrugstorewater hiccups
fun a nice sissy under me clean and whistling a donkey to ride rocks
                "OKAY (smile) COMING UP"
"This is, after all," said Margaret Dumont, "the *original* MAIN CHANCE"
(fart) "Suck this," said the Old M, spitting on his high heels
which he had just put on to get his navel up to her knee

but even that extended a little further,
        out into the desert, where
        no flash tested, no flashed!
        oops! and no nail polish, yak
                        yak, yak, Lieut.
        no flesh to taste no flash to tusk
        no flood to flee no fleed to dlown flom the iceth loot
"par exemple!"

out of the dark a monster appears full of grizzly odors which exhale through
him like a samovar belches out the news of the Comintern in a novel by
Howard Fast
        BUT
                      the cuckoo keeps falling off the branch so everything's okay
nobody worries about mistakes disasters calamities so long as they're "natural"
sun sun bene bene bullshit   it's important to be sensitive in business and
insensitive in love because what have you if you have no "balls" what made
the French important after all if not: jeu de balles, pas de balles and,
for murderers of Algerians, règle de balles   may I ask
                 "do you love it?"

   I don't think I want to win anything I think I want to die unadorned

        the dulcet waves are
        sweeping along in their purplish
        way and a little girl is
        beginning to cry and I know
        her but I can't help because
        she has just found her first brick
        what can you do what

does that seem a little too Garboesque? now Garbo, a strange case. oh god

keeping them alive
        there are more waves with bricks in them than there are
                well-advertised mansions in the famous House

but we will begin again, won't we

                                       well I will anyway or as 12,
       "continuez, même stupide garçon"

                 "This dedelie stroke, wherebye shall seace
                 The harborid sighis within my herte"

and at the doorway there is no
                 acceptable bong except stick mush
room for paranoia comme à l'heure de midi moins quatre
                         et pour
JOUR DE FÊTE j'ai composé mon "Glorification" hommage au poète américain
       lyrique et profond, Wallace Stevens
                           but one
       of your American tourists told me he was a banker
                       quels délices
     I would like to tell you what I think about bankers but . . .
                except W. C. Fields

what do you want from a bank but love   ouch
           but I don't get any love from Wallace Stevens no I don't
I think délices is a lot of horseshit and that comes from one who infinitely
                    prefers bullshit
               and the bank rolled on
               and Stevens strolled on
               an ordinary evening alone
               with a lot of people

           "the flow'r you once threw at me
           socked me with hit me over the head avec
           has been a real blessing let me think
           while lying here with the lice
                   you're a dream"

AND

"measure shmeasure know shknew
unless the material rattle us around
pretty rose preserved in biotherm
and yet the y bothers us when we dance
                                        the pussy pout"
                    never liked to sing much but that's what being
                            a child means   BONG

le bateleur! how wonderful
I'm so so so so so so so so so so happy
so happy I make you happy
like in the s- s- s- s- soap opera wow
            what else I mean what else do you need (I)
                                        then you
                        were making me happy otherwise I
                        was staring into *Saturday Night* and flag
                        pink shirt with holes cinzano-soda–grin
                        unh. it is just too pleasant to b.w.y.

hey! help! come back! you spilled your omelette all over your pants!
oh damn it, I guess that's the end of one of our meetings

"vass hass der mensch geplooped
that there is sunk in the battlefield a stately grunt
and the idle fluice still playing on the hill
because of this this this this slunt"
                                it's a secret told by
                                a madman in a parlor car
                                signifying chuckles
                                    * Richard Widmark *
                                    * Gene Tierney *
                                    * Googie Withers *

            I hate the hat you are not wearing, I love to see your narrow head

there in the dark London streets
                            there were all sorts of murderers
                  gamblers and Greek wrestlers
         "I could have had all of wrestling in London in my hand"
           BANG
                            down by the greasy Thames shack
                            stumbling up and over

                  (PROKOFIEVIANA)
One day   you are posing in your checkerboard bathing trunks
      the bear eats only honey   what a strange life

is the best of mine impossible   what does it mean

            that equally strange smile it's like seeing the moon rise
                "keep believing it"
        you will not want, from me

      where you were no longer exists
      which is why we will go see it to be close to you how could it leave

I would never leave you
if I didn't have to
              you will have to too
              Soviet society taught us that
              is the necessity to be "realistic" love is a football
                    I only hear the pianos
           when possession turns into frustration
           the North Star goes out will it
           is there anyone there
the seismograph at Fordham University says it will
                      so it will not

              we are alone no one is talking it feels good
      we have our usual contest about claustrophobia
      it doesn't matter much
      doing without each other is much more insane

okay, it's not the sun setting it's the moon rising
I see it that way too

(BACK TO SATIE)

when the *Vitalità nell' arte* catalog came in the mail I laughed
                    thinking it was *Perspectives USA* but it wasn't it
                    was vitality nellie arty ho ho that's a joke pop
                    "I never had to see I just kept looking at the pictures"
                                        damn good show!
                                        don't I know it?
                                        take off your glasses
                                        you're breaking my frame
                                        sculptresses wear dresses

    Lo! the Caracas transport lunch with George Al Leslie 5:30 I'll
be over at 5
                    I hope you will I'm dying of loneliness
                    here with my red blue green and natch pencils and the erasers
                    with the mirror behind me and the desk in front of me
                    like an anti-Cocteau movement
"who did you have lunch with?" "you" "oops!" how ARE you

                    then too, the other day I was walking through a train
                    with my suitcase and I overheard someone say "speaking of faggots"
                    now isn't life difficult enough without that
                    and why am I always carrying something
                    well it was a shitty looking person anyway
                    better a faggot than a farthead
                    or as fathers have often said to friends of mine
                    "better dead than a dope" "if I thought you were queer I'd kill you"
                    you'd be right to, DAD, daddio, addled annie pad-lark (Brit. 19th C.)

                    well everything can't be perfect
                    you said it

    I definitely do not think that Lobelia would be a suitable name
for Carey and Norman's daughter if they have a daughter

and if they have a son Silverrod is insupportable by most
put that back in your pipe Patsy and make pot out of it honey

you were there I was here you were here I was there where are you I miss you
(that was an example of the "sonnet" "form") (this is another)
when you went I stayed and then I went and we were both lost and then I died

                                oh god what joy
                                you're here
                                sob and at the
                                most recent summit
                                conference they
                                are eating string
                                beans butter
                                smootch slurp
                                pass me the filth
                                and a coke pal
                                oh thank you

down at the box-office of Town Hall I was thinking of you in your no hat
        music often reminds me of nothing, that way, like reforming

September 15 (supine, unshaven, hungover, passive, softspoken) I was
very happy
                on Altair 4, I love you that way, it was on Altair 4 "a happy day"
                I knew it would be
                yes to everything
                                I think you will find the pot in the corner
                where the Krells left it
                                        rub it a little and music comes out
                the music of the fears
                                        I reformed we reformed each other
                being available
                                        it is something our friends don't understand
                if you loosen your tie
                                        my heart will leap out
                like a Tanagra sculpture
                                        from the crater of the Corsican "lip"

and flying through the heavens
                              I am reminded of Kit Carson
and all those smiles which were exactly like yours
but we hadn't met yet
                              when are you going away on "our" trip
why are you melancholy
                        if I make you angry you are no longer doubtful
if I make you happy you are no longer doubtful
                                        what's wrong with doubt

it is mostly that your face
is like the sky behind the Sherry Netherland
blue instead of air, touching instead of remote, warm instead of racing
you are as intimate as a "cup" of vodka
                    and when yesterday arrives and troubles us you always say NO
                    I don't believe you at first but you say no no no no
                    and pretty soon I am smiling and doing just what I want
                    again
                                    that's very important
                                    you put the shit back in the drain
                                    and then you actually find the stopper

take back September 15 to Aug something
I think you are wonderful on your birthday
                                    I think you are wonderful
        on all your substitute birthdays
                              I am rather irritated at your being born
                              at all
                              where did you put that stopper
                        you are the biggest fool I ever laid eyes on
                        that's what they thought about the Magi, I believe

first you peel the potatoes
then you marinate the peelies
in campari all the while playing
the Mephisto Waltz on your gram

and wrap them in grape leaves
and bake them in mush ouch
that god damn oven delicacies
the ditch is full of after dinner

                    what sky
                    out there in between the ailanthuses
                    a 17th Century prison an aardvark
                    a photograph of Mussolini and
                    a personal letter from Isak Dinesen
                    written after eating

            the world of thrills! 7 Lively Arts! Week-in-Review! whew!
            if you lie there asleep on the floor after lunch
            what else is there for me to do but adore you
            I am sitting on top of Mauna Loa seeing thinking feeling
            the breeze rustles through the mountain gently trusts me
            I am guarding it from mess and measure
                                        it is cool
                                        I am high
                                        and happy
                                        as it turns
                                        on the earth
                                        tangles me
                                        in the air

the celestial drapery salutes an ordinary occurrence
the moon is rising I am always thinking of the moon rising
                            I am always thinking of you
                                your morality your carved lips
            on the beach we stood on our heads
            I held your legs it was summer and hot
            the Bloody Marys were spilling on our trunks
            but the crocodiles didn't pull them
            it was a charmed life full of
            innuendos and desirable hostilities
            I wish we were back there among the
            irritating grasses and the helmet crabs
            the spindrift gawk towards Swan Lake Allegra Kent

those Ten Steps of Patricia Wilde
unison matches anxious putty Alhambra
bus-loads of Russians' dignity desire
when we meet we smile in another language

you don't know the half of it
I never said I did
your mortality
I am very serious

ENDGAME WAITING FOR GODOT WATT HAPPY DAYS which means I love you
what is that hat doing on that table in my room where I am asleep
"thank you for the dark and the shoulders"
"oh   thank you"

okay I'll meet you at the weather station at 5
we'll take a helicopter into the "eye" of the storm
we'll be so happy in the center of things at last
now the wind rushes up nothing happens and departs
L'EUROPA LETTERATURA CINEMATOGRAFICA ARTISTICA 9-10
your back the street   solidity   fragility erosion
why did this Jewish hurricane have to come
and ruin our Yom Kippur

favorites: vichyssoise, capers, bandannas, fudge-nut-ice, collapsibility,
    the bar of the Winslow, 5:30 and 12:30, leather sweaters, tunafish,
    cinzano and soda, Marjorie Rambeau in *Inspiration*
                    whatdoyoumeanandhowdoyoumeanit

(MENU)
Déjeuner Bill Berkson
30 August 1961

Hors-d'oeuvre abstrait-expressionistes, américain-styles, bord-durs, etc.
Soupe Samedi Soir à la Strawberry-Blonde
Poisson Pas de Dix au style Patricia
Histoire de contrefilet, sauce Angelicus Fobb

La réunion des fins de thon à la boue
Chapon ouvert brûlé à l'Hoban, sauce Fidelio Fobb
Poèmes 1960-61 en salade

       Fromage de la Tour Dimanche 17 septembre
       Fruits des Jardins shakspériens
       Biscuits de l'*Inspiration* de Clarence Brown

Vin blanc supérieur de Bunkie Hearst
Vin rouge mélancholique de Boule de neige
Champagne d'*Art News* éditeur diapré
Café ivesianien "Plongez au fond du lac glacé"
                 Vodka-campari et TV

as the clouds parted the New York City Ballet opened Casey Stengel was there
with Blanche Yurka, "Bones" Mifflin, Vera-Ellen and Alice Pearce, Stuts
"Bearcat" Lonklin and Louella "Prudential" Parsons in another "box," Elsa
"I-Don't-Believe-You're-a-Rothschild" Maxwell wouldn't speak to them
because she wasn't "in" the party and despite the general vulgarity Diana
Adams again looked exactly like the moon as she appears in the works of
Alfred de Musset and me
               who am I? I am the floorboards of that zonked palace

after the repast the reap (hic) the future is always fustian (ugh)
   nobody is Anglican everybody is anguished

"now the past is something else the past is like a future that came through
you can remember everything accurately and be proud of your honesty you can
lie about everything that happened and be happily reminiscent you can alter
here and there for increased values you can truly misremember and have it
both ways or you can forget everything completely the past is really something"

       but the future always fall' through!
       for instance will I ever really go live
       in Providence Rhode Island or Paestum Lucania
       I doubt it   "you are a rose, though?" (?)

a long history of populations, though
the phrase beginning with "Palms!" and quickly forgotten

in the pit under the dark there were books
being written about strange rites of the time
the time was called The Past and the books were in German
which scholars took to be Sanskrit or Urdu
(much laughter) which later turned out to be indeed
Sanskrit or Urdu (end of laughter, start of fight)
and at the same time the dark was going on and on
never getting bluer or greener or purpler just
going on and that was civilization and still is
nobody could see the fight but they could hear what
it was about and that's the way things were and stayed
and are except that in time the sounds started to
sound different (familiarity) and that was English

        well, that Past we have always with us, eh?
        I am talking about the color of money
        the dime so red and the 100 dollar bill so orchid
        the sickly fuchsia of a 1 the optimistic
        orange of a 5 the useless penny like a seed
        the magnificent yellow zinnia of a 10
        especially a roll of them the airy blue of a
        50 how pretty a house is when it's filled with them
        that's not a villa that's a bank
        where's the ocean
now this is not a tract against usury it's just putting two and two together
            and getting five (thank you, Mae)

    actually I want to hear more about your family
            yes you get the beer

I am actually thinking about how much I love Lena Horne
I never intended to go to New Hampshire without you
you know there's an interesting divinity in Rarotonga that looks sort of like you

"I am a woman in love" he said
the day began with the clear blue sky and ended in the Parrot Garden
the day began and ended with my finding you in the Parrot Garden

Lena Horne had vanished into a taxi and we were moreorless alone together
of course it wasn't Lena Horne it was Simone Signoret we were happy anyway

"As if a clear lake meddling with itself
　　Should cloud its pureness with a muddy gloom"

"My steeds are all pawing at the threshold of the morn"

favorites:　going to parties with you, being in corners at parties with you,
　　　　　being in gloomy pubs with you smiling, poking you at parties when
　　　　　you're "down," coming on like South Pacific with you at them,
　　　　　shrimping with you into the Russian dressing, leaving parties with
　　　　　you alone to go and eat a piece of cloud

　　　　　　　　YIPE! 504 nails in *The Gross Clinic*!
　　　　　　　　it's more interesting to see a Princess dance
　　　　　　　　with a Bluebird than just two bluebirds
　　　　　　　　dancing through diagonal vist' together

at the flea circus there was a bargain-hunter
at the end of the road a bum, the blue year
commenced with an enormous sale of loneliness
and everyone came back with a little something
one a baby, one a tooth, one a case of clap
and, best of all, a friend bought a medical dispensary
there were a lot of limbs lying around so
of course someone created a ballet company, oke
the barely possible snow sifted into a solid crystal
I sometimes think you are Mozart's nephew: "Talk
to me Harry Winston, tell me all about it!"

　　　　　　　　"from August to October
　　　　　　　　the sun drips down the sign
　　　　　　　　for eating at midnight ask Virgo
　　　　　　　　to be lost outside the cafeteria"

　　　　I went to Albania for coffee and came back for the rent day

"I think somebody oughta go through your mind with a good eraser"
meanwhile Joe is tracing love and hate back to the La Brea tar-pits

hear that rattling?
those aren't marbles in my head they're chains on my ankles

why do you say you're a bottle and you feed me
the sky is more blue and it is getting cold
last night I saw Garfinkel's Surgical Supply truck
and knew I was near "home" though dazed and thoughtful
what did you do to make me think
after we led the bum to the hospital
and you got into the cab
I was feeling lost myself

(ALWAYS)

never to lose those moments in the Carlyle without a tie

endless as a stick-pin barely visible you
drown whatever one thought of as perception and
let all the clouds in under the yellow heaters
meeting   somewhere over St. Louis
call me earlier because I might want to do something else
except eat   ugh

endlessly unraveling itself before the Christopher Columbus Tavern
quite a series was born   as where I am going is to
Quo Vadis for lunch
out there in the blabbing wind and glass   c'est l'azur

perhaps
marinated duck saddle with foot sauce and a tumbler of vodka
picking at my fevered brain
perhaps
letting you off the hook at last or leaning on you in the theatre

215

oh plankton!
"mes poèmes lyriques, à partir de 1897, peuvent se lire comme un journal intime"

yes always though you said it first
you the quicksand and sand and grass
as I wave toward you freely
the ego-ridden sea
there is a light there that neither
of us will obscure
rubbing it all white
saving ships from fucking up on the rocks
on the infinite waves of skin smelly and crushed and light and absorbed

A BRIEF CHRONOLOGY
OF FRANK O'HARA'S LIFE AND WORK

1926	Born on June 27, in Baltimore.
1927	The family moved to Grafton, Massachusetts.
1933–44	Attended parochial schools in Worcester.
1944–46	Served as sonarman third class on the destroyer USS *Nicholas.*
1946–50	Continued his studies in music at Harvard College, then changed his major to English; B.A. 1950. Published poems and stories in the *Harvard Advocate.*
1950–51	Entered Graduate School of the University of Michigan; M.A. 1951. Received Hopwood Award in Creative Writing. The Poets' Theatre, in Cambridge, produced his plays *Try! Try!* and *Change Your Bedding.* In New York City he was employed by the Museum of Modern Art.
1952	*A City Winter, and Other Poems,* his first book of poems, was published by Tibor de Nagy Gallery.
1953–55	As an editorial associate of *Art News* he wrote reviews and occasional articles.
1955	Rejoined the Museum of Modern Art. As a special assistant in the International Program he organized many important traveling exhibitions.
1957	*Meditations in an Emergency* published by Grove Press.
1958	Universal Art Editions published *Stones,* the lithographs he made with Larry Rivers.
1959	*Jackson Pollock* published by George Braziller. *Love's Labor, an Eclogue* produced by the Living Theater.
1960	*Odes,* with serigraphs by Mike Goldberg, published by Tiber Press; *The New Spanish Painting and Sculpture* published by Museum of Modern Art. *Awake in Spain* produced by the Living Theater. Appointed Assistant Curator of Painting and Sculpture Exhibitions.
1961	Served as art editor of the quarterly *Kulchur.*
1962	Received a grant from the Merrill Foundation.
1963	Conducted a poetry workshop at the New School for Social Research. Collaborated with Al Leslie on the film *The Last Clean Shirt.*
1964	*Lunch Poems* published by City Lights Books. *The General Returns from One Place to Another* produced at the Writer's Stage Theatre.
1965	*Love Poems* published by Tibor de Nagy; *Robert Motherwell* published by Museum of Modern Art. Appointed Associate Curator. Collaborated with Al Leslie on the film *Philosophy in the Bedroom.* Featured in the National Educational Television *USA: Poetry Series.*
1966	Wrote introductions for the *David Smith* and *Nakian* catalogs published by the Museum of Modern Art. On July 25th he died as the result of injuries sustained in an automobile accident. He was buried in the Springs cemetery, near East Hampton.

D . A .

Poem   (for Don
                        Christmas 1959)

Now the violets are all gone, the rhinoceroses, the cymbals
a grisly pale has settled over the stockyard where the fur flies
and the sound
                is that of a bulldozer in heat stuck in the mud
where a lilac still scrawnily blooms and cries out "Wait!"
so they repair the street in the middle of the night
and Allen and Peter can once again walk forth to visit friends
in the illuminated moonlight over the mists and the towers

having mistakenly thought that Bebe Daniels was in I Cover the Waterfront
instead of Claudette Colbert it has begun softly to rain and I walk
slowly thinking of becoming a stalk of asparagus for Hallowe'en
          which idea Vincent proposes as not being really '40s
so the weight
                of the rain drifting amiably is like a sentimental breeze

and seems to have been invented by a collapsed Kim Novak balloon

yet Janice is helping Kenneth appeal to the Ford Foundation in
her manner oft described as the Sweet Succinct and he'd so glad
          not to be up too late
                          for the sake of his music and his ear
                when discipline finds itself singing and even screaming
I shall not dine another night like this with Robin and Don and Joe
as lightly as the day is gone but that was earlier
                                        a knock on the door
my heart your heart
                my head and the strange reality of our flesh in the rain
so many parts of a strange existence independent but not searching
                                        J in the night
                nor in the morning when the rain has stopped

                                        —Frank

INDEX OF TITLES AND FIRST LINES

Poem titles are printed in italic type

Index of Titles and First Lines

A NOTE ABOUT THE EDITOR

Donald Allen grew up in northwest Iowa and was educated at the state universities of Iowa, Wisconsin, and California (Berkeley). After wartime service in the Navy in the Pacific, Washington, and London, he worked for ten years in publishing in New York City. Since 1960 he has made his home in San Francisco, where he directs the Four Seasons Foundation and Grey Fox Press. He has translated *Four Plays of Eugène Ionesco,* and has edited the following: (with Francisco García Lorca) *The Selected Poems of Federico García Lorca; The New American Poetry;* (with Robert Creeley) *New American Story* and *The New Writing in the USA;* (with Warren Tallman) *The Poetics of the New American Poetry;* and *The Collected Poems of Frank O'Hara.*

A NOTE ON THE TYPE

The text of this book was set on the Fotosetter in a type face called Biretta—the camera version of Bembo, the well-known monotype face. The original cutting of Bembo was made by Francesco Griffo of Bologna only a few years after Columbus discovered America. It was named for Pietro Bembo, the celebrated Renaissance writer and humanist scholar who was made a cardinal and served as secretary to Pope Leo X. It was in recognition of Pietro Bembo's role as cardinal that the name Biretta was chosen for the film adaptation of the face.

Sturdy, well balanced, and finely proportioned, Bembo is a face of rare beauty. It is, at the same time, extremely legible in all of its sizes.

The book was composed by Westcott & Thomson, Inc., Philadelphia, Pennsylvania, and York Graphic Services, Inc., York, Pennsylvania. It was printed and bound by Kingsport Press, Inc., Kingsport, Tennessee. Typography and binding design by Betty Anderson.